Jack Hill's
COUNTRY CHAIR
MAKING

Jack Hill's
COUNTRY CHAIR MAKING

David & Charles

NOTE ON MEASUREMENTS

All measurements of length used in this book are given in imperial sizes, expressed in inches and fractions thereof, followed by the generally accepted metric equivalent in millimetres. This is a cumbersome but necessary dichotomy; all the chairs described and shown were made to imperial measurements because that is the system I use and the one in which I think. Metric sizes are given for those who work, and think, in that system, but it should be clearly understood that these are approximate and not precise equivalents. The two systems should not be intermixed.

A David & Charles Book

Copyright © Text, line drawings and designs Jack Hill 1993
Colour photographs John Plimmer 1993
First published 1993

Jack Hill has asserted his right to be identified as author of this work in accordance with the Copyright, Designs and Patents Act 1988.

A catalogue record for this book is available from the British Library.

ISBN 0 7153 8767 7

Typeset by ICON, Exeter
and printed in Italy by Milanostampa SpA
for David & Charles
Brunel House Newton Abbot Devon

CONTENTS

INTRODUCTION

'Country chairs' is a general term used to describe those simple, sometimes sturdy, yet often quite elegant chairs made originally by village craftsmen during the eighteenth and nineteenth centuries. Made for use in cottage and farmhouse, they were the inspiration of a pre-factory age when individual interpretation and regional differences prevailed. Largely uninfluenced by the dictates of fashion and changing taste, they retained their traditional, functional form throughout. In later years some were made in urban as well as rural areas, and as demand increased, many were made in factories. Thus the term 'country' chair may seem inappropriate, and alternative names are sometimes used to distinguish these plain, vernacular chairs from the more elaborate and stylish chairs which graced the drawing-rooms and dining-rooms of the wealthier households. My preference remains, however, as I see them as 'country' in origin.

Broadly speaking, country chairs may be divided into two distinctive groups: the first, and the earliest in use, are those of an open frame construction usually with woven or sometimes panel seats and made with either a ladderback or a spindleback. Ladderback chairs take their name from the ladder-like arrangement of horizontal slats between the two back uprights, while spindlebacks have vertical rows of short turned spindles between pairs of horizontal back-rails. Seats are usually of woven rush, but willow was also used, and straw, and some had thin wooden panel seats.

The second group embraces all those chairs which have a solid, shaped wooden seat with legs socketed into it from below, and separate top components arising from it above to form various back arrangements: comb-back, bow-back, and so on. Generically described as 'Windsor' chairs, they were in fact made in many areas and this regional attribution is something of an inveterate misnomer.

There are considerable differences between these country-made chairs and those made earlier and concurrently in the furniture-maker's workshops, usually from seasoned oak, with their heavy 'joyned' frames, all morticed and tenoned and too angular for comfort. The country makers abandoned oak in favour of other native woods – notably strong and flexible ash – and to simplify construction, used turned components with round dowels fitting into round sockets. An explanation for this radical change lies in the fact that these rural chairmakers were primarily woodturners and possibly wheelrights, and their methods were developed out of existing, traditional rural skills basic to their own and other woodland and coppice trades. For well over a hundred years these craftsmen made their chairs, partly out in the woods where their material grew, and partly in village workshops, utilising their native skills and the simple technology of the time.

Sadly, social change and increasing demand saw the demise of the majority of these country chairmakers and their individual workshops. The factory system which replaced them meant standardisation, machined parts assembled on a production-line basis, and a corresponding loss of craftsmanship and honesty. By the early part of the present century few truly traditional chairmakers remained, and as working methods were not written down but passed on orally from father to son, master to apprentice, the practical skills and 'tricks of the trade' were in danger of disappearing altogether.

Tenuous links remained, however, and due partly to a resurgence of interest in country crafts and craftsmen of all kinds – albeit a somewhat romanticised interest in many respects – sufficient information became available to make it worthwhile for continued research and practical study by a number of individuals, including myself, into old working methods, tools, devices, materials, and so on. Today, therefore, encouraged by an increased awareness of the sound craftsmanship inherent in so many traditional crafts, country chairmaking is enjoying a healthy revival among many workers in wood. This book is my contribution to that revival.

My own interest in traditional crafts in general and country chairs in particular began in the early 1970s, an outcome of which was my first book *Complete Practical Book of Country Crafts*, published in 1979. Since that time, looking at old chairs, restoring them, making new ones and teaching others how to make them has contributed to the body of knowledge and experience which I now share with you.

The scheme of this book is in two parts. Part One starts with a brief history of the development of chairs and a pictorial description of the rural chairmakers in their woodland and village workshops. Next it goes on to the more practical issues of materials, tools and

Country chairs

devices, and working methods (techniques), all of which are pertinent to the projects which follow. Part Two comprises the projects; these are more or less chronologically arranged, and graded from easy to make to more difficult. This part begins, in fact, with designs for stools, the stool being the basis of country chair construction.

To many woodworkers, even experienced cabinet-makers, chairmaking is seen as a complicated business, fraught with problems of compound angles, awkward joints, curved components, and little which is 'square' to serve as a reference base. Working drawings in conventional plan and elevation are pointless; the carpenter's square is useless. Popular hearsay describes how old chairmakers did everything 'by hand and by eye', and there is no doubt that many did work in this way – I well know that the ability to do so is very satisfying and does help in some procedures. But ability of that kind only comes with experience, and

experience not only takes time but it must have a beginning – a period of 'doing' before it is acquired.

Consequently the methods described, while based firmly upon traditional ways of working, are rationally augmented by the use of simple jigs and devices and some modern tools which make the work less physical and more predictable, and provide useful aids to accuracy. Because this eliminates many of the apparent problems in chairmaking, it brings the work well within the skill ability of a wide range of people, from the raw beginner and college student, to the enthusiastic amateur, the semi- and full-time professionals, and even the experts. Much of the 'mystique' of chairmaking is therefore removed, and whilst I have not been able to describe every minute detail, I hope that the information contained here is adequate and useful, and that it helps you to make a chair, then a better chair, and then more chairs even better.

CHAIRS AND CHAIRMAKERS

Chairs were not a part of domestic furniture in England until about the middle of the sixteenth century. Before that time chairs were not unknown in the medieval manor house but there was rarely more than one, and this would be reserved for the exclusive use of the lord or master of the house. Lesser members of the household sat on low stools or benches; in the poorer dwellings everyone sat on stools.

The seat as a symbol of status has prevailed throughout history, from primitive tribes and Egyptian pharaohs to today; witness our present use of the title 'chairman' (or its modern euphemism chairperson) for someone who presides over a corporate company or a meeting of the village committee. The origin of the word 'chair' has its roots in the Latin *cathedra* meaning seat; hence cathedral is, literally, 'the seat of the bishop'.

The medieval chairs were 'chairs of estate': large, throne-like, pretentious and too heavy to move around. It is claimed that they developed from the ubiquitous wooden chest, probably by extending upwards a high-panelled back and lower sides which formed armrests. They were made in oak and were of 'joyned' construction, for this was the Age of Oak and the time of the joiner.

Sixteenth century joined oak armchair

Sixteenth century joyned stool in oak

Many of the stools and benches of the period were similarly of oak and 'joyned', all furniture at that time being based upon a rectilinear 'case' construction consisting of substantial vertical posts or stiles and horizontal rails, all right-angled and joined with pegged mortice-and-tenon joints. For chests and chairs the interspace was panelled; for tables and stools it was left open. In the wealthier households the 'joyned' stools would be embellished with turned legs and carved top rails, although the boarded seat still provided little or no comfort. There was yet another type of stool, more commonly found in the poorer cottages and farmhouses of the countryside: it was different in construction insofar as it had a solid wooden seat with three, sometimes four legs socketed into angled holes bored through from underneath. The work of village woodturners, the three legs were more stable on the uneven stone or hard earth floors.

An alternative chair design was the 'X'-frame chair; this was once the prerogative of kings but was reintroduced and eventually came into popular use. However, a more interesting development was the

A late seventeenth century thrown chair

appearance of the so-called 'thrown' chair: 'thrown' as in pottery meaning 'shaped whilst revolving', in other words a chair turned on a lathe. Sometimes called a bobbin chair, it is entirely different to the 'joyned' chair both in concept and construction, for turned components and round dowel joints predominate. Said to be thirteenth century and Byzantine in origin, the few extant examples – probably eighteenth century – display a 'frenzy of turning'. They were made three-legged and four-legged to give both triangular and rectangular seats, and in contrast to the closed, 'joyned' chair they were fashioned in an open frame construction.

The work of woodturners using the primitive pole lathe, some were made in ash and others in elm, both easier to turn than oak; and it is probably no coincidence that this chair re-emerged when there was bitter dispute between the guilds of carpenters, joiners and turners as to who should do what. Hitherto turners had made parts for joiners to joint and assemble, but when some joiners began doing their own turning, some turners began making their own chairs.

Meanwhile the common bench had been elevated to the communal settle by the addition of a high boarded back; and in due course some 'joyned' stools were given backrests by the simple expedient of extending one pair of legs upwards above the seat and then infilling the two stiles with a back panel. The addition of a back not only improved comfort but also suited the female dress fashion of the time, the farthingale. To preserve the dignity and status of those who still enjoyed the

Seventeenth century Derbyshire chair (or backstool)

Seventeenth century Yorkshire chair (or backstool)

privilege of the 'chair of estate', these new-fangled chairs were not at first regarded as 'proper' chairs but were known as 'stoole with a back' or backstools. As they developed further they were eventually accepted as chairs, and as a result several regional styles emerged. Most important amongst these were the Derbyshire chair with its arcaded top rail and spindle back, and the Yorkshire style with its back of two, sometimes three, carved cross-rails.

As well as the problems of identity experienced by the furniture-makers, both taste and the traditional ideas of patronage were also changing, reflecting the social upheaval and foreign influences of the time. Carved ornamentation proliferated, and upholstery was popularised; and later, cane seating was introduced, causing further 'distress in the trade'. These events had their principal effects upon the furniture-makers who supplied the wealthier classes of the cities and towns, since for these, furniture had become fashionable rather than merely functional. In the country, however, the village carpenter or turner, or whatever, continued to make all manner of things, as he always had done, to suit his customers' more utilitarian needs.

As a consequence, what appears to have been a divergence of interest in furniture development took place. While makers in London and other centres of population followed the dictates of fashion and foreign influence, those in the countryside – and there was a lot more of it then – adhered more to their native traditions. Rural isolation and poor communications restricted the interchange of ideas and innovation, with the result that, whilst there was occasional infiltration, country furniture styles tended to evolve locally and separately.

Nowhere is this more obvious than in the differing methods of making chairs, and in the different styles of chair produced. The chairs which were to replace the simple stools and benches in cottage and farmhouse, and 'below stairs' in the larger households, broke away almost completely from the joiner's rectilinear, mortice-and-tenoned form of construction; moreover these makers used not oak, but ash, elm and other woods for preference. Primarily the work of woodturners and wheelwrights, the choice of material and the various patterns of working were in fact a natural continuation and adaptation of their existing, traditional skills.

Of paramount significance in all this was the way these craftsmen made use of mature and coppice wood, and their technique of working it whilst still green (ie unseasoned), often cleaving, shaping and turning it out in the woodland where it grew. Such methods had been followed for centuries by woodland workers who made fence posts, gates and hurdles; by ladder-makers

and rake-makers; and for producing tool handles of all kinds. Shaping parts by steam-bending had its precursors, too: boat-builders, scythe snaith (handle) makers, barrel-makers. The emerging country chairmakers simply followed these same practices, adapting and developing them for their own purposes.

The earliest country chairs were of a simple open-frame construction, possibly a development of more humble stools with woven seats, but with positive design links back to the turner's 'thrown' chair, certainly in their construction and jointing methods. Made almost entirely of turned parts similarly socketed together, these links become less tenuous when extant examples of the American 'Brewster', 'Carver', and early slat-back chairs are taken into account, assuming a similar process of evolution. These open-frame chairs had back legs extending above the seat, and two quite distinct back arrangements evolved: the spindleback, with its row (or rows) of vertical, turned spindles between curved back rails; and the ladderback, which has a number of broad horizontal bars or slats. Each has

Seventeenth century American slat-back chair

design references back to the aforementioned Derbyshire and Yorkshire style chairs.

Ash was the material most commonly used in making these chairs. It was abundant as coppice in many areas of Britain, and it was the first to be chosen in other woodland crafts where qualities of strength and resilience were required; it was therefore both an appropriate and an economic choice for chairs – wherever they were made, the two requirements of hard use and cheapness still had to be met.

Seats were most often woven with rush, an aquatic plant whose usefulness had been exploited for centuries for a variety of purposes. When twisted together and woven onto the chair frame it provided an inexpensive, renewable and comfortable seat. In areas where willow was more plentiful this was used instead; whilst in rural Ireland, plaited straw made the seat of the súgán chair. An alternative but harder seat was made from a thin wooden board slotted between the seat rails – a further link with the 'thrown' chair which had a similar seat.

In the early days of chairmaking it is likely that the traditional method of cleaving and turning green wood would simply have been extended so that it was the unseasoned components which were assembled into chairs, and what is more, without using glue. Such methods had always been adequate for tool handles, rakes, gates, cartwheels, and so on. But these were all used outdoors, and furthermore rakes and suchlike could occasionally be soaked in the farm trough, and cartwheels wetted in the village pond or ford – Constable's painting 'The Haywain' is witness to this. But for use indoors, even in the poorly heated and often damp rural dwellings of the time, the wood in the chairs would have dried out and joints become loose, and even if they were occasionally given a dip in the village pond or left out in the rain, continued use and wear would inevitably result in the chairs quite literally falling apart.

Consequently working methods were modified: the procedure adopted was evidently to continue to take advantage of the ease of cleaving, shaping and turning the wood in its green, unseasoned condition, but then to allow components time to dry out before the jointing and assembly stages. Also, a glue made from waste animal hides and bones was used. Later, when power-driven machinery was introduced, sawn, seasoned wood was used.

The second distinctive group of country chair appeared at a later date. These were almost certainly developed out of the simple three- and four-legged cottage stools. With angled legs socketed into their solid seat from below, the metamorphosis into chair was brought about by adding a back consisting of spindles, and a cross-rail, similarly socketed into the seat from above, to make what would at first have been a transitional backstool.

It is not at all clear when this process began; there are what could be prototypes in some primitive West Country, Welsh and Irish 'stick-back' chairs, but the evidence is poor. What *is* clear is that the chair type was at a fairly advanced stage of development when it first appeared, most probably in the county of Buckinghamshire, and was apparently already known by its present name, the 'Windsor' chair. Speculation about the origin of this name suggests an association with the forest or town of Windsor in Berkshire, perhaps as a market centre for such chairs sold to London dealers. Later, High Wycombe was to become a centre for their manufacture, founded upon the dominant tree of the surrounding Chiltern hills, the beech. But all Windsor chairs were not made in High Wycombe, nor were – or are – they made exclusively from beech.

The first Windsors were of the comb-back variety, having a series of back spindles and, sometimes, outer stiles surmounted by a shaped top rail known as a cresting or comb. Some had a curved back rail which not only provided armrests, it strengthened the back; on the earliest chairs this was built up from separate parts, and not made in a continuous bend as it was later. Legs were turned or shaped with the drawknife and widely splayed for stability, without stretchers. Initially they appear to have been very popular as garden chairs.

When steam-bent arm-bows appeared, the comb was soon replaced by a top- or back-bow to produce what is now known as the hoop-back or double bow Windsor; and in due course another style developed in which a longer and sturdier bow was socketed down into the seat, producing the single bow Windsor. And there are other variants: the Gothic, the smoker's bow, the wheelback and several others with distinct regional characteristics, as well as a number of American interpretations.

Alongside these Windsor chair developments, ladderback and spindleback chairs were to undergo a series of stylistic changes too, and distinctive regional types developed. By the beginning of the nineteenth century, however, the various types and styles of country chair in England seem to have reached an evolutionary plateau; they continued to be made – and later in vast numbers – but with little, if any change from then on.

Little is known about the early rural makers of ladderback and spindleback chairs, but it is likely that they worked as individuals or in family groups in simple workshops which were perhaps part of, or nearby, the cottages in which they lived. They would have cut coppice locally, cross-cutting it to required lengths and either cleaving and turning it out in the woods where it grew, or carting it back to their workshops to do so. Unlike the Windsor chairmakers, those who made ladderbacks and spindlebacks appear to have made complete chairs, from start to finish, including the rush seating in many cases. Finished chairs were assembled using animal glue, but their success (and this is equally applicable now as then) lay in well-fitting joints and their 'box' construction, engineered so that resilient, individual, tensioned components contributed to the chair's overall strength and stability.

One of the few documented early makers of these chairs was Philip Clissett: born in 1817 into a family of chairmakers, from about 1840 he had his own workshop in the village of Bosbury in Herefordshire. For most of his working life he made mainly spindleback chairs with inset wooden seats (page 120), a traditional style of that part of the West Midlands region; it was not until he was in his seventies that he appears to have made the rush-seated ladderbacks with which his name is closely associated (page 88). This transition appears to have taken place in about 1886 when Clissett met the architect James Maclaren. Later, another architect, Ernest Gimson, a devotee of the hand craftsmanship ideals of William Morris, went to work with Clissett to learn from him the basic skills of his craft, and it was this association which gave the old man his place in the annals of furniture design.

Gimson subsequently made, or had made, rush-seated chairs to his own designs (page 114), incorporating, it seems likely, features recently found to have been used by another chairmaking family, the Kerry family of Worcestershire. Whatever the truth of the matter, the fact remains that the recognition of, and the interest in the work of Philip Clissett, and others, has led to a valuable link with past practices, for it is well known that Gimson encouraged a young Edward Gardiner to make chairs, and that one of Gardiner's several apprentices, Neville Neal, continued to make them after Gardiner himself died in 1958. Neal's son continues to make chairs to designs by both Clissett and Gimson to the present day.

The Windsor chairmaking tradition which began later is much better documented and was altogether different. Few Windsors were made completely from start to finish by one man – they were usually made piecemeal by several, the work most often divided between that done in the woods, and that done by others in a workshop.

The first of these, the turners, would set up their pole lathes under rough shelters set out in the woods, and then fell coppice and mature trees which they cut

Philip Clissett in his workshop

Chair 'bodgers' working out in the woods early this century

to required lengths. These would be split or cleft into segments with an axe, or with wedges and a heavy mallet known as a beetle. On a chopping block and using a side axe – an axe only bevelled on one side – these segments were trimmed to a roughly hexagonal shape, bark and pith being removed in the process. Next came the first stage in shaping and rounding: this was done on the shaving horse, a foot-operated vice device which grips the wood tight, and using a sharp drawknife the piece was made almost round, and ready for turning on the lathe.

The turners used few tools at the lathe – a broad skew chisel, a gouge and a beading tool were all that most of them needed. Leg turnings varied in pattern both chronologically and regionally, these individual features now providing a useful clue to identification. Finished legs and the stretchers which would brace them were stacked, criss-cross fashion, outside to dry and season.

The lifestyle of these woodland turners, or 'bodgers' as they have become known, was – and to some extent still is – over-romanticised, working as they did among the trees, communing with nature and all that kind of

thing. The truth of the matter is that these turners had to work hard and fast to make a living. There are no records earlier than the beginning of this century, but at that time a bodger received only 5s (25p) for each gross of legs (a gross was twelve dozen, that is 144) plus the appropriate number of stretchers (108). To earn a decent living wage of 12s 6d per week (62p) meant they had to make a total of 756 turned parts.

The origin of the name 'bodger' is obscure, and there is no evidence that it was applied until the present century. The same name was given to itinerant pedlars, whilst the German cooper (barrel-maker) is a *bottcher*, and an alternative spelling of 'bodger' is *bojjer*. In modern usage, 'bodger' (also spelt 'botcher') is a derogatory name given to someone who does a bad job – or isn't it someone who never completes a job? (The Windsor turners rarely completed a chair.) To add to the confusion, some who today style themselves 'bodgers' offer complete chairs for sale. However, I suspect the name has been popularised as part of the romantic myth.

Traditionally the bodger either sold his products to a dealer, or direct to a workshop where several men would continue the work, a system of 'division of labour' predating production-line methods in other industries. The work would be divided between *bottomers* who cut and shaped chair seats using a long-handled adze; *benders* who cut and steam-bent the required bends or bows; *benchmen* who made additional parts, and bored the holes for joint sockets (using only a brace and bit); and *framers* whose job it was to make tight-fitting joints and assemble the various components into the complete chair. Early Windsors were finished by painting – green seems to have been a popular colour; later they were stained and polished. In smaller workshops, some of the work allocations described might have been combined.

The late eighteenth and early nineteenth centuries saw a period of unprecedented change throughout most of England as it evolved from a largely rural economy into an industrial one. Populations not only increased, they became more centralised as people migrated in huge numbers from the countryside into consequently fast-growing urban conurbations. The population of London almost doubled between 1801 and 1831, and in the county of Lancashire in the same period it rose from about 674,000 to 1,400,000.

Chair manufacture became a thriving business as it tried to keep pace with the increasing demands which these changes created. Inevitably it increasingly became factory based, and with the introduction of steam power many of the processes were mechanised. The outcome was an increase in the standardisation of components, and as competition grew, a decrease in quality and individuality. Where ladderback and spindleback production had once been quite separate from Windsor chairmaking, many factories now combined their manufacture for wider distribution, and regional characteristics began to disappear. Social change brought about new tastes in fashion, and demand moved away from traditional styles to the Victorian 'fancy' chairs in carved mahogany, imitation bamboo, and caned and upholstered seats. And so the true country chair was first mechanised, then standardised, and finally commercially bastardised.

Fortunately, a few rural makers in scattered communities had continued to work as they had always done. Paradoxically a demand for certain components made from cleft material carried on, in particular for Windsor legs and stretchers – Government contracts still specified this throughout World War II. Among the last woodland woodturners making such Windsor legs were the brothers Owen and George Dean. Owen continued to work among the trees until the 1950s, his pole lathe set up inside a wooden shed. He claimed that he could still turn ten to twelve dozen (120–144) legs and stretchers in a day's work, this routine occasionally relieved by making school rounders bats. Another, Samuel Rockall, still working in 1960, had

Owen Dean splitting beech billets

A High Wycombe chair factory in the early twentieth century

Owen Dean working at the shaving horse

Owen Dean working at the pole lathe

Completed chair legs stacked to season

been a chair turner for over sixty years, although he turned on a treadle lathe.

There were others, but few are recorded. This is likewise true of individual chairmakers and although painstaking research by Dr Bernard Cotton is revealing more and more information, the only well-documented chairmaker is H.E. 'Jack' Goodchild who lived and worked at Naphill in Buckinghamshire until he died in 1950. Unusually he made Windsor chairs from start to finish, apparently combining the work of bodger, bottomer, bender and benchman – as I do now, and describe here.

Although his workshop was simple and cluttered, Jack Goodchild's workmanship was first class; in later life, however, he became the focus of attention in a period of intense interest in rural living, and in which the country craftsman was idealised. Some writers of that period portrayed such people as quaint relics of the past, living out their lives in some rural idyll 'hand in hand with nature in a world in which machinery, progress and money play little or no part'. In the event, however, it was this somewhat morbid interest which, reinterpreted, provides such useful insights into the many aspects of the working methods of the past.

Jack Goodchild adzing a chair seat

Jack Goodchild drilling leg sockets in a chair seat

Jack Goodchild fitting a back splat

Jack Goodchild 'legging up'; fitting legs into a seat

Jack Goodchild staining completed chairs

MATERIALS

Wood is the predominant material used in making chairs. Whether this is obtained direct from the tree out in the woods, or indirectly from the sawmill or timber merchant, is a matter of availability and personal circumstances.

Some may already have, or have access to, material in a woodland source. Coppicing is again being carried out on a small scale in some areas – in a few it never ceased – whilst in places where trees are managed, thinnings and clearances are a likely source, as of course are windblown trees. Voluntary groups are often involved in work of this kind, and participation can be doubly rewarding. A close alternative to this direct approach is to obtain material at secondhand from similar sources, by begging it or buying it as round logs or poles in suitable sizes: estate forestry yards, farmers and firewood dealers can be most helpful. Any of these sources can provide the opportunity to begin work using green (unseasoned) wood and to experience the ease with which it can be cleft and shaped and turned.

It is appreciated, however, that this may not be possible in all cases and that the material most easily available will be sawn timber bought from a timber merchant. Such material is quite suitable; it was used in the past in the later mechanised workshops, and indeed it is used on my own chairmaking courses where, because of the short time-span of the course, after practice in using green wood, seasoned material is used to make components for a finished chair because there is then no risk of shrinkage. It is true that seasoned wood is harder to work than unseasoned wood, but with sharp tools and powered lathes and turning devices this is not a problem.

When purchasing timber in this way there may be a choice between air-dried or kiln-dried wood. Use air-dried where it is available, and select straight-grained material, especially when using it for slender components and for steam-bending purposes. Air-dried timber is from trees which, after felling, are sawn into boards and stacked, separated by spacer sticks, to season naturally over a long period in the open air but protected from rain and too much sun. It is available at many sawmills and is to be recommended; for steam-bending it is essential for satisfactory results. Kiln-dried timber is artificially dried, either in heated kilns or by a process of dehumidification. Where only kiln-dried timber is obtainable, it can be used for turned components and for Windsor seats, but it is not generally suitable for steam-bending.

An important criterion in chairmaking is the selection of material, and using those species of tree which have the required properties. The properties required of wood used in chairmaking, in the case of frames for ladderbacks and spindlebacks and in Windsor chairs (except seats), are strength and resilience ie it must be strong and flexible with a high resistance to shock stress. Where in other woodland crafts these same properties had been required, the first choice was always ash, and its use in chairmaking was therefore a natural outcome over most of Britain where the tree is native and common. In one particular region where beech is the dominant tree this was used instead; several other species had minor use in other areas.

For wooden chair seats, particularly those of Windsor chairs, the required properties are rather different. Strength is still needed, but a high resistance to splitting is of major importance – thus the wheelwright's choice for wheel-hubs or naves became the chairmaker's choice for seats: this was elm, a strong, durable timber whose interlocking grain gives it the correct characteristics. Elm is also native to Britain, and was once widespread; sadly it is fast disappearing due to the ravages of Dutch elm disease.

18

ASH Common or European ash, *Fraxinus excelsior*, is a hardwood native to Britain and grows throughout the country. Coppice and other young growth is best for chair-work – mature trees can be used, but they tend to go brown and become brittle through the centre. Trees from about 8in (200mm) to about 12in (305mm) in diameter at head-height are the most suitable if straight-grown and knot-free.

Fairly quick-grown ash is best – eight to ten growth rings per inch (25mm) is ideal. Ash cleaves readily, and is easy to work and turn when green. It becomes harder when dry, but turns and finishes well with sharp tools.

It is one of the best woods for bending after steaming. Straight grain is of prime importance, and part-dried cleft material is preferable, although sawn, straight-grained air-dried material can be used. American ash varieties, *F. americana* and others, are suitable for chairmaking but are normally available in Britain only as seasoned sawn boards.

BEECH Beech, *Fagus sylvatica*, is a hard, strong wood but it lacks the toughness and resilience of ash. It is an even-textured and generally stable wood, which wears well and can be readily stained. Beech cleaves easily, although material from older trees can become fibrous and difficult to work. On the lathe it turns well both green and when dry. It bends readily after steaming if selected for straight grain. Windsor chairmakers in Buckinghamshire used beech almost exclusively as it was abundant in that area. Imported (European) beech is also suitable for chair-work.

The even texture of beech results from its annual growth pattern. The pores produced by the cambium are very fine and evenly distributed and there is little if any distinction between winter and summer growth. Its ray figure, however, is distinctive and shows as tiny flecks on cut surfaces.

YEW Among the other trees used in chair-work, yew (*Taxus-baccata*) is the most significant. Botanically a softwood, it has properties of strength and toughness which make it superior to most other softwoods and many hardwoods. Its appearance, too, makes it a desirable material and it was always a favourite choice for 'best Windsors'. Slow-growing, it produces a dense wood often with a wild grain which makes it difficult to cleave. However, it turns well to a hard, smooth finish, and straight-grained material can be bent after steaming. For this latter purpose young, straight branchwood and sapling growth is best.

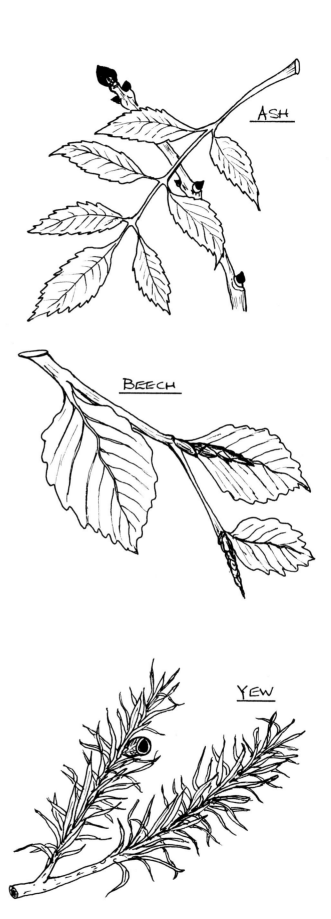

BIRCH The varieties of birch *Betula pendula* and *B. pubescens* have often been used in making chairs, although much more frequent use was, and still is, made of this species elsewhere, particularly in Scandinavia. It turns easily, green or dry, and can be brought to a good finish. It is not unlike beech to work, perhaps a little softer.

CHERRY The wild cherry, or gean (*Prunus avium*) is also suitable for chair-work: the wood is reddish-brown in colour, sometimes with greenish streaking, and has a close, fine texture; it can be a little brittle to work when seasoned, but it turns well, green or dry.

APPLE AND PEAR Of the other so-called fruitwoods, the apple (*Pyrus malus*) and the pear (*Pyrus communis*) are found as components in chairs. Their close grain and even texture make them equally satisfactory for this use – if they can be found in suitable sizes. Both turn well and take a good finish.

HAZEL More a bush than a tree, hazel (*Corylus avellana*) is still coppiced in a number of areas and can be used successfully to make a number of slender chair components. It cleaves readily and bends easily.

SYCAMORE Sycamore (*Acer pseudoplatanus*) is a member of the maple family; its wood resembles beech in its main properties, and it is used in furniture-making, as well as having a number of craft uses. It cleaves readily, it turns well both green and when dry, and it can be bent after steaming although it is a little brittle.

OAK The oak *Quercus robur*, and other varieties and cultivars, are native to and common throughout Britain. Oak is, of course, a very strong timber except when fast-grown, but it is heavy, hard to work and lacks the flexibility of ash. It bends easily and takes a good finish, and is used in chair-work.

American oaks, differentiated in the timber trade as red and white, are available as sawn, seasoned boards in Britain.

SWEET CHESTNUT The sweet chestnut (*Castanea sativa*) is common in southern England. Superficially it resembles oak in colour, and contains the same tannic acid which blackens and can corrode tools when these woods are worked green. But it is lighter in weight than oak and not so hard or durable. It cleaves readily and is easy to shape and turn, especially when green.

ELM The English elm (*Ulmus procera*) and wych elm (*U. glabra*), together with their several hybrids, were once abundant in Britain, and the wood from these trees with its interlocking grain is ideal for Windsor chair seats. Sadly, the ravages of Dutch elm disease have caused the rapid demise of almost all the elm trees in Britain – odd pockets still remain, but probably not for long. Immune varieties are being bred and planted, but even if they survive, there will be a 100-year absence of mature elms. American elm, also in limited supply, is still obtainable in Britain, but only in narrow boards.

There appears to be no real substitute for elm; if it is not available, then almost anything else is worth trying. Wide boards of brown-hearted ash have been used successfully, while others have tried beech and oak, although both of these are heavy; in the USA several different pine species are used. Where wide boards are unobtainable, seats may have to be made up by edge-gluing narrower boards.

WOVEN SEAT MATERIALS The most common of these is rush, *Scirpus lacustris*, an aquatic plant found along the margins of some lakes and slow-flowing rivers. It is harvested annually, and the 6–8ft (2–2.5m) stems are dried and sold in bundles or bolts or by weight. Before it is used it has to be made pliable by damping with water; it is then skilfully twisted and tightly woven across the chair-seat rails to a traditional pattern. A cheap substitute for rush is the material known as 'seagrass'. This grows in the Far East and is imported, already mechanically twisted into long continuous lengths, and sold by the hank. It can be woven to the same pattern as rush, and is quick and convenient, but it is not authentic on country-made chairs.

Basket maker's willow or osier (*Salix triandra*), and others, is suitable for seat-weaving and was once used in willow-growing areas. It can be bought dry as brown, white and buff willow, the latter being the most suitable. An early type of chair in rural Ireland, the súgán chair, had a woven seat of straw or hay – súgán is Gaelic for *straw*; this was plaited into a rope before being woven across the seat from side to side.

Other materials used in seat-weaving, more common in the USA, are oak 'splits': these are obtained by splitting or riving thin pliable strips of coppiced oak, or by peeling the inner bark of certain trees into narrow strips – in parts of America, hickory and ash are used; in Britain, elm and lime have been tried. The American Shaker communities made seats of coloured woven tape about 1in (25mm) wide which was woven across the seat rails often using two contrasting colours to form a chessboard pattern. The Shakers wove tape specifically for this purpose.

FINISHING MATERIALS: Completed chairs require a 'finish' of some kind, not just for the sake of appearance but for surface protection and to seal the pores of the wood. The most common finish is wax polish, a mixture of beeswax and turpentine and perhaps other minor ingredients, obtainable under several proprietary names. Before the wax polish is put on, what is generally known as sanding sealer may be applied, either shallac- or ethanol-based, first to seal and, when sanded, then to smooth open grain. Various oil finishes may be used: linseed, tung, Danish, and so on. Where it is required to darken the wood, stains or wood dyes can be used; a wide range of these is available. Some early chairs were painted and there has been a revival of interest in paint as a finish.

A row of mature elms, now a rare sight in our countryside

TOOLS AND DEVICES

The tools of the traditional country chairmaker were few and simple, in keeping with the technology of the time. Some remain unchanged, still in use and available today, but others were home-made devices or the product of a local blacksmith which were never made commercially. Occasionally these and other old tools may be purchased second-hand, but if they are 'collectable' they can be rare and costly. Modern tools may be used where possible, and this includes power tools – these can certainly save unnecessary, difficult and perhaps repetitive work, provided this does not denigrate the workmanship.

TOOLS FOR WOODLAND WORK

For the initial woodland work, all that was required was a crosscut saw, an axe, some wedges and perhaps a froe, a heavy mallet, a side axe and a drawknife plus a few turning tools. In the workshop a frame saw, an adze, a travisher and scrapers, and a range of boring tools, a bow saw, spokeshaves, a couple of chisels and a framer's hammer were enough for the majority of the work.

SAWS AND AXES

The **crosscut** would often be a two-man saw, though nowadays a 30in (760mm) metal-frame **bow-saw** does the job well enough; or of course a **chainsaw** can be, and is, frequently used. After felling and sawing to length, the **axe** and **heavy mallet** are used to split the short billets. The axe is used in the manner of a wedge with a handle, and struck by the mallet which is usually a short-handled, home-made affair ringed with iron bands to prevent it splitting. Such a mallet was known as a **beetle**, meaning 'a tool for beating'. Longer billets are cleft lengthways, using the axe together with wedges to extend the splitting action.

The **froe** is a useful tool employed in a number of woodland crafts, its name deriving from the archaic English word 'froward', the opposite of 'toward' (hence the expression 'to and fro'). It is an L-shaped tool consisting of a substantial blade attached at right-angles to a short wooden handle. Its cutting edge faces down and away from the user, and its back can be struck with a mallet if necessary; or it is used with a levering action to extend a running split usually in a

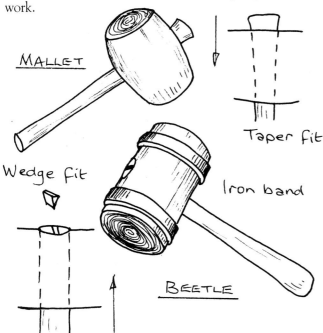

MALLET

Taper fit

Wedge Fit

Iron band

BEETLE

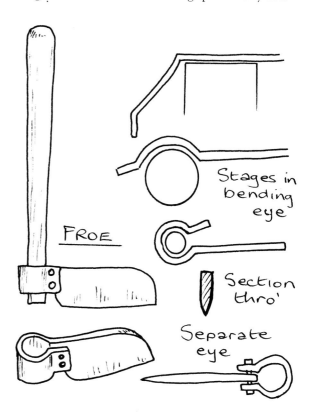

FROE

Stages in bending eye

Section thro'

Separate eye

22

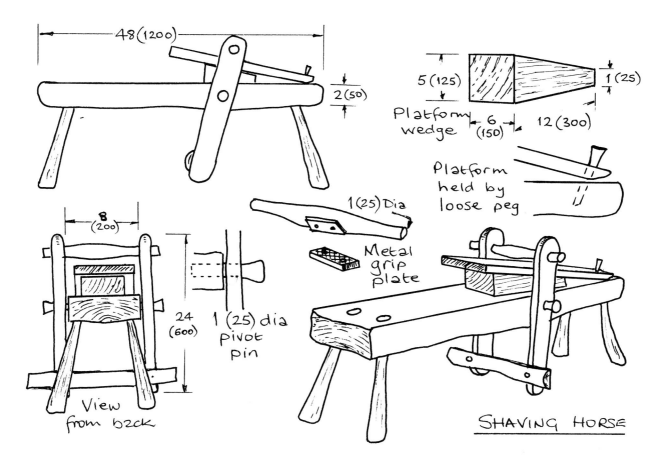

5 (125) 1 (25)

Platform wedge 6 (150) 12 (300)

48 (1200)

2 (50)

Platform held by loose peg

8 (200)

1 (25) Dia

Metal grip plate

24 (600)

1 (25) dia pivot pin

View from back

SHAVING HORSE

long, small-diameter coppice pole. The froe was the product of a local blacksmith, and instructions are given for its making, and for making the beetle too.

After the cleaving operation, the **side axe** is used to trim the clefts, at a thigh-high chopping block. This axe is unlike the normal pattern in that it is bevelled and sharpened on one side only; used flat-side to the work, it comes in left-hand and right-hand versions. With its usually short, curved handle it is easy to control, and its chisel-like cutting action enables the user to trim wood with considerable accuracy. At the time of writing (1992) the side axe is no longer being manufactured in Britain but an imported one is available and occasionally old ones can be found second-hand.

TOOLS FOR CUTTING AND TURNING

The **drawknife** is still available both new and second-hand. This tool is suitable for roughing out work and for fine shaving and shaping, and provided it is kept razor sharp and its handler has a little practice, it was – and still can be – used in numerous wood crafts to do many jobs. It works extremely well on green wood. Double-handled and bevelled along one edge only, it can be used either way up – the bevel to, or away from the work. In the former position I find I have more

control over the cutting edge, but this is a matter of personal choice. Several sizes of drawknife are available new, but I prefer a good old one of medium size.

If a gadget or a device could be made to simplify their work, the old country craftsmen made it and used it, choosing to waste neither time nor effort in unnecessary toil. They seem to have been particularly adept at making holding devices, and several kinds of 'break' were made; one such device was the **shaving horse** (or mare, mule or donkey), and this became, together with the drawknife, an indispensable combination in so many country crafts in Britain and elsewhere. Its design details vary, but its main function is as a kind of foot-operated vice, to hold wood for shaping against the pull of the drawknife. The worker sits astride the horse facing an adjustable, wedged platform and a pivoted swinging arm, and by pushing with the feet against a lower crossbar of the swinging arm, the opposite movement of a top crossbar pinches the workpiece between it and the platform. This grips the workpiece firmly, yet allows it to be easily and quickly moved to a new position as required, leaving both hands free to use the drawknife efficiently. The diagram shows how to make a shaving horse.

The **pole lathe** was also used in a number of crafts and trades, and had been in use since primitive times; it derives its name from the long springy pole which helps drive it. The motive power is provided by the thrust of the turner's leg through a foot treadle; attached to the treadle is a cord which goes up, around the workpiece which would be held between fixed centres, but free to rotate, and on up to be attached to the tip of the overhanging springy pole. The butt end of the pole is anchored firmly at ground level, and there is an intermediary fulcrum. Thus when the treadle is pressed, the cord is pulled down and the workpiece revolves – the pole bends like a fishing rod, only to spring back up again when the pressure is released. The pole in effect acts as a return spring, the workpiece revolving first forwards then backwards – the 'power' stroke as the treadle is pressed, followed by the return stroke of the unbending pole. Wood can only be cut on the power stroke as the workpiece revolves towards the turner.

Modern power-lathe operators would consider this reciprocal motion, the lack of power and speed, and the physical effort required to be a severe limitation. However, in the hands of a skilled operator this is not the case, and the pole lathe can be an efficient device and a pleasure to use when working green wood; but it lacks the power required for turning seasoned wood, and it isn't everyone's idea of fun! The diagram shows how one can be made.

Four turning tools, plus a **bradawl** for marking centres, are all that are required in turning green wood on a pole lathe: a wide (1in–1½in/25–38mm) **gouge** for initial cuts; a wide (1½–2in/38–50mm) **skew chisel** for smoothing; a **smaller skew** (½in/12mm); and a small (⅜in/9mm) **spindle gouge** for beading and other decoration. If you choose to use a **powered lathe** – and many of us do – the same tools will suffice for both green and seasoned wood.

TOOLS FOR THE WORKSHOP

In the workshop the different procedures require different tools and techniques, and in later years various kinds of machinery came into use. Originally the **frame-saw** would have been used for cutting out Windsor chair seats, from boards laboriously sawn at the saw-pit; now this is more likely to be done on a **bandsaw**, where one is available. A heavy-duty electric **scroll-saw** will do the job, but only just and perhaps not for long; and if you have to work by hand, a

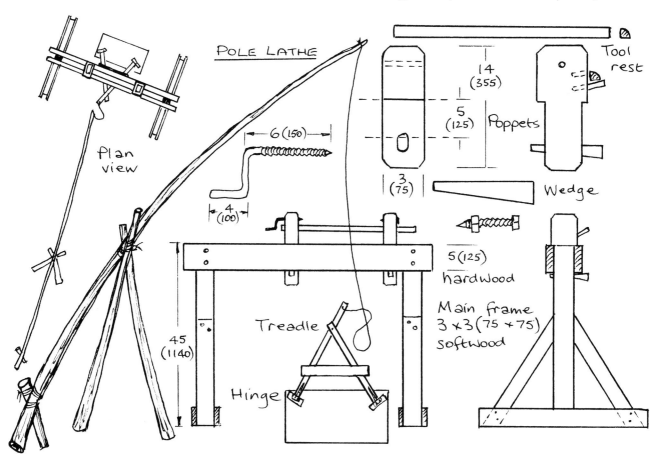

wooden frame, cord-tensioned **bow-saw** is perfectly adequate.

Hollowing or bottoming the seat was traditionally done with a long-handled **adze**, the seat held to the floor and the adze swung with a scooping action to rough out the seat shape. New long-handled adzes are still offered for sale, but they are not the chairmaker's type which should be double-curved like a wood-carver's **spoon gauge**. Such a gouge in a large size can be used instead of an adze: it should be struck by a mallet, working in the manner of carving a shallow bowl. A short-handled curved **carver's adze** may also be used. In the USA the **gutter adze** is used by some chairmakers.

For smoothing the rough surface left by these methods, a wooden-handled tool called a **travisher** was normally used, but these are no longer made and second-hand ones are very rare. An alternative which *is* available is a Sheffield-made, double curved sole, steel **spokeshave**. Also useful – and available – is an **inshave**, a two-handed tool which resembles a deeply curved drawknife. It is most efficient when kept properly sharp, and I often use one to hollow a Windsor seat from beginning to end, needing only to finish off with a curved scraper: a slow method but a safe one!

Eventually there were – as indeed there still are – machines for commercial seat shaping, For smaller enterprises and individual work, various mechanical alternatives are currently advocated: the tips of chainsaws; high speed routers in elaborate jigs; or a recent innovation, the Arbortech woodcarver which I do use myself occasionally. These methods may be quick if you care to live dangerously, but they are risky both to oneself and to the wood – and they are certainly anti-social!

BENDING WORK

For bending work the following are required: a **boiler** in which to raise steam, connected to a suitable **container** in which to place the wood being bent. The old workshops usually had a stove burning waste wood which heated water in a tank enclosed by a brick or metal **steam-'box'**. An alternative method is suggested here (see diagram), using readily available standard materials. For the actual bending, **formers** or **bending forms** of the required type, size and shape are needed, and these, too, are simple enough to make; dimensions and shapes are obtained from the relevant diagrams given in Part Two.

Windsor bow formers can be permanently fixed to plain back-boards, or made to be interchangeable and used together with the bending 'table' shown overleaf. In use these are held to a substantial bench by means of cramps.

Formers for ladderback and spindleback chairs are normally gripped in a bench vice. Note that all items made and used for bending work should be particularly well constructed to withstand the stresses imposed upon them in use.

Marine grade plywood
←10 (250)→ ½ (12)

10 (250)

2½ kw Kettle element inside metal container

60 (1500)

Section thro' box

Condensation

STEAMER

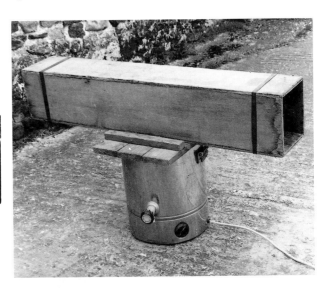

Boiler and steam box

In former times a bending table (see illustration) was necessary for bending Windsor bows, as the bend was made by pegging and wedging these around the former on the table; this may still be done, but to reduce the risk of breakage it is now more common to use the table in conjunction with a **bending or supporting strap.** The diagram shows how these can be made, and their use is described on page 36. Large-scale commercial bending is done using pressurised steam treatment and hydraulically operated, multiple-bending machines.

DRILLING AND CUTTING

Holes for joint sockets were at one time judged simply by eye, and bored by hand, using the wooden stock-brace and spoon-bits of the time. **Spoon-bits** are an effective means of making chair joint sockets, but went out of fashion; however, they are available again and may be used in the carpenter's **hand-brace.** A variety of other bits (or drills) can be used, favourite among them being the **spiral auger bit.** These are particularly

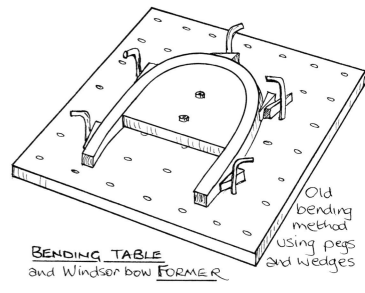

BENDING TABLE and Windsor bow FORMER

Old bending method using pegs and wedges

Formers for ladderback and Spindleback chairs

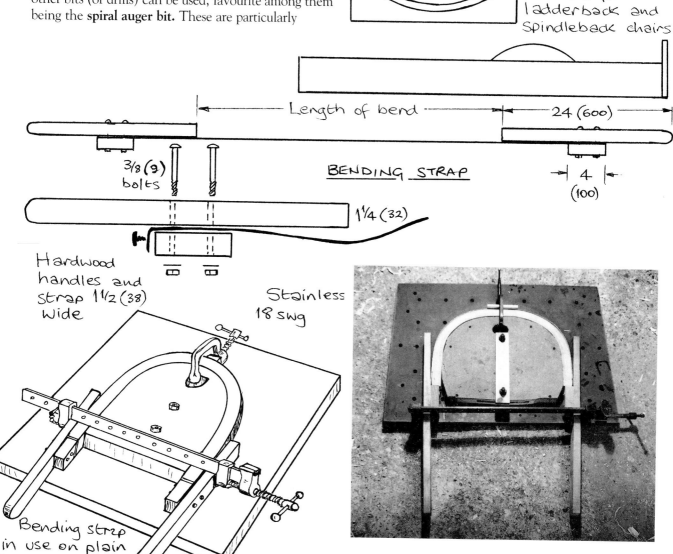

Length of bend

24 (600)

3/8 (9) bolts

BENDING STRAP

4 (100)

1¼ (32)

Hardwood handles and strap 1½ (38) wide

Stainless 18 swg

Bending strap in use on plain bending table

Bending table with bent bow in position in bending strap

effective in green wood, but for boring 'blind' holes they are not ideal, nor are any other bits which have lead screws.

To bore holes accurately for joint sockets, and at a variety of angles, by hand and using eye judgement only, was a highly skilled job, and it was one of the first to be mechanised in the early chair workshops. This was not to increase production, but to decrease costs by bringing the work within the capability of less skilled workmen. For similar reasons, the use of an **electric drilling machine** in conjunction with the drilling jigs shown is recommended. The machine can be a portable **hand-drill** held in a drill-stand, or it can be a **bench** or **pedestal drill** or **drill press.** The method provides not only a mechanical means of making socket holes, but also a fixed reference for accurate angle and compound-angle drilling when used with the jigs shown here and described on page 39

The drilling bits most suitable for use with this method are the machine, **saw-tooth, Forstner-type bits;** they make clean, accurate, parallel-sided, flat-bottomed sockets, ideal for the 'socket and round tenon' construction which is the basis of country chairmaking. The four most useful sizes are ½in (12mm), ⅝in (16mm), ¾in (19mm), and 1in (25mm).

For the measurement and setting of angles, a carpenter's **sliding bevel square** and **protractor** may be used, or an inexpensive **'angle finder'** can be obtained. This incorporates a bubble or spirit level in a rotatable bezel, and can be set at any angle between 0° and 90°.

Spirit-level type angle finder

27

The slot mortices for back-slats in ladderback chairs may be cut by hand, or be made by other means. Chain-drilling by hand or machine, followed by careful chiselling is effective. Various router bits are available if a router is used, but the most suitable tool is one made specially for the job, the two-wing **chairmaker's mortice bit** (see page 41). The ¼in (6mm) size is required; it has a ½in (12mm) shank and will not fit most small routers. The bit works best when operated at about 6,000 RPM, but I use one quite successfully in a bench drill at about 4,000 RPM.

Other components such as combs, centre back-splats, arms and curved back-slats were once cut out by hand-saws of various kinds; now, a **band saw** or **jig-saw** may be used. The above components, and also bent bows after drying, require further shaping. Initially this may have been done with the drawknife, but for final shaping and smoothing, spokeshaves with wooden stocks in various sizes – some straight, some curved – would have been used, followed by scrapers which were often made from bits of broken saw-blade.

The **spokeshave** is a versatile tool and is still in use, but it is now most often seen with an iron stock and in one size only. However, these are reasonably adequate if kept sharp and adjusted correctly. New wooden stock spokeshaves can still be bought but only in one size; individual blades of different curvature are obtainable for fitting to home-made wooden stocks. Of course, old spokeshaves can still be found and are worth searching for; these must also be kept sharp and properly adjusted if they are to cut efficiently. Steel scrapers are readily available, and learning how to sharpen one is well worth the time.

MISCELLANEOUS

Other miscellaneous tools might include a small (¼in/ 6mm) and a larger (¾in/19mm) **bevel-edge chisel** (for hand-cutting centre splat and back-slat mortice slots and trimming wedges); a **small sharp knife,** for all kinds of trimming and whittling; and a **hammer** and a **soft mallet** for use at the assembly stage. This soft mallet can be one with a hide or composite rubber head.

THE FRED LAMBERT SYSTEM

As already mentioned, a powered lathe can be used for turning, and most people would probably choose to work in this way, especially, for example, when making Windsor chair legs and stretchers. Some may encounter problems, however, when they need to make longer components by this means: problems of long slender components 'whipping'; problems of

restricted lathe bed length when dealing with even longer ladderback and spindleback back uprights. To overcome this sort of thing, I chose to adopt a system of turning – or 'rounding' as I prefer to call it, to distinguish the method from true turning – pioneered by the late Fred Lambert: Fred's system entirely eliminates these difficulties, and provides an alternative, safe method of working which is suitable for those less skilled at, or not in possession of, a lathe.

Fred based his ideas on the wooden **rounders** or **rotary planes** once used in several woodland and village crafts (for example in rake- and besom-making, ladder-making and wheelwrighting), developing a series of tools in cast aluminium with brass insets and adjustable (spokeshave) cutters which made it easy to produce consistently-sized 'dowels' of literally any length. These tools may also be used to size accurately the round tenons used in chair construction. (Tools known as **hollow augers**, once available in America, were at one time used for the latter purpose.) Fred called his tools **rounders,** and they were made in several sizes together with an additional tool, the equivalent of the old 'stail engine' and which he named a **trapping plane,** capable of producing long tapered shapes and therefore ideal for chair spindles.

Fred tutored courses in making and using these tools specifically for educational purposes, and this was how I came to meet him and to adopt his methods, initially for teaching purposes in schools, and then for my own work and college courses. For the past eighteen years I have used successfully both the tools and the methods, with young children and disabled teenagers and in colleges and on courses with adults; with beginners and experts alike; ladies as well as men. Many adult students have gone on to adopt the system for themselves.

For hand-work, wood is held in a vice and the

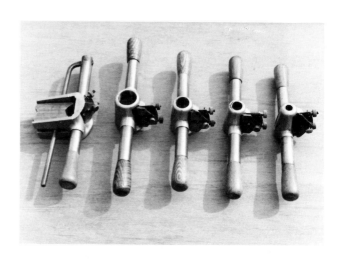

A chairmaker's set of the Fred Lambert rounders

Rounder in use in vice

rounder rotated around it (see above). An alternative and quicker method is to have the wood revolving slowly through the tool; a simple, hand-turned device can be used to do this, or a **'rounding machine'** can be assembled to do the work mechanically and more efficiently. For tapering, the wood must normally be revolved.

The photographs of these tools in use here and on page 33 should be fairly self explanatory; the diagram below shows the basic principle of a rounding machine. The tools, the gear-box rounding machine parts, and the instructions for manufacture, as well as complete machines ready to go, are all exclusively made and available from the address given on page 147. Slow speed machining using these tools is emphasised; 150 to 250 RPM is sufficient and safe. Note that the lowest spindle speed on most commercial lathes is usually too fast, so beware. Some variable speed lathes *can* go slow enough, but at the time of writing lack sufficient torque at these low revolutions.

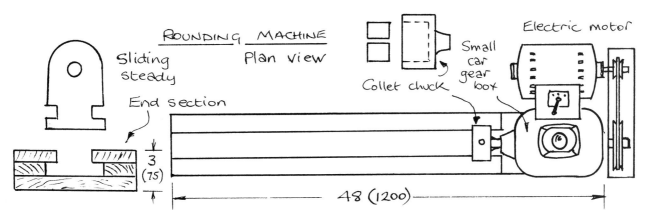

Techniques

We have seen that there are different types and styles of country chair, and that their methods of construction may vary; however, in general terms and within the context of the two distinct groups of ladderback/spindleback types and Windsor types, they can all be made by following similar basic principles.

Preparing The Wood

UNSEASONED WOOD

Common to all is the initial work in the preparation of material. Where this is green, unseasoned wood in the round log form, it must first be cut to the required lengths – billets should always be cut a little overlength to allow for discolouration or for any end splitting. Lengths initially sawn at 6ft (2m) long are most convenient, being long enough for Windsor bends and suitable for resawing economically to other required lengths: a generous two-thirds for ladderback back uprights; in half for front uprights; and into slightly unequal thirds for most other things – Windsor chair legs and back spindles, stretchers and seat-rails, ladderback arms and back-slats.

The shorter lengths are cleft in an upright position using the axe and heavy mallet, first in half, through the heart, then radially, usually into quarters or perhaps six depending on size. These clefts may then be further reduced to suit the work in hand, including cleaving tangentially *ie* with the growth rings. Avoid using wood where the heart lies well off-centre, as this is due to uneven growth and the wood will be stressed and problematic. Longer lengths are split horizontally on the ground: start with the axe on the edge of one end, then extend the split with wedges. When a long length of straight-grained material has been split into two halves it can be rip-sawn or bandsawn, flat surface to the saw-table, into its required sizes if you choose and if such facilities are available.

Splitting coppice logs for chair legs

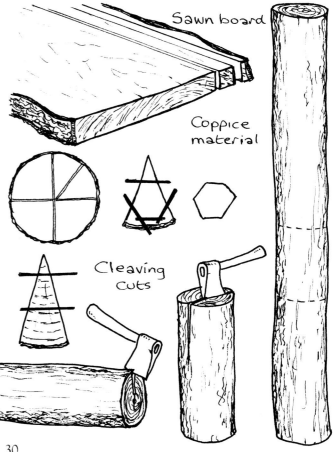

Sawn board

Coppice material

Cleaving cuts

SEASONED WOOD

Where the wood used is seasoned, sawn material bought in as waney-edge boards, first select the thickness required, then saw (or have sawn) one edge square and proceed to saw off the sections needed according to the appropriate cutting list given in Part Two. Alternatively, material may be bought in ready sawn in the required sizes and sections. Be generous with length measurements, but more accurate with section dimensions, especially if rounders are to be used.

WOOD FOR BENDING AND SHAPING

For bending purposes, choose wood with the straightest grain. If it is cleft, select it from the outside of the tree where it is youngest and most pliable. Mark the wood selected for bending, and put it to one side until ready to use. There are advantages in allowing green wood to dry a little – and disadvantages if wood of any kind becomes too dry.

The trimming and shaping of green wood clefts depends upon their ultimate use and how they will be worked; pick generous sizes whatever their purpose, to allow for wastage. If using a pole lathe, the secret of success lies in the use of green wood and its correct preparation almost to its finished diameter before it

Sawn board ready for use

The shaving horse in use

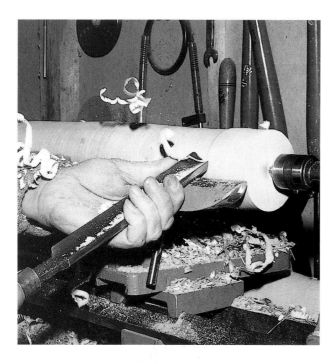

Roughing out on the conventional lathe

goes on the lathe. First, trim with the side axe, if you have one, ideally at a firm chopping block about thigh-high, and initially to a roughly hexagonal shape. Then shape this on the shaving horse more towards round, keeping in mind the final size and shape desired. For all lathe-turned parts, pole-operated or by power machines, the finished diameters will vary, but the shape will usually be a cylinder tapering slightly to both ends. Short lengths are easy enough, but with longer lengths on the shaving horse the excess should lie over the knee and under the arm whilst the drawknife is applied. On the lathe, component-length will cause other and perhaps greater problems.

ROUNDERS

Long components need not be lathe-turned; they can be shaped just with the drawknife and left with that finish, or they can be cleaned up by scraping. Alternatively they can be entirely shaped with the Fred Lambert rotary planes or rounders. If rounders are to be used, then the preparation of green wood need not be too precise; simply bring it to a size which will fit the tool. Sawn wood may be cut square to the sizes given.

Rounders may be used entirely by hand to 'turn' or round wood to accurate diameter and any length, and in a variety of sizes dependent upon the specific tool used. The tools leave a good surface finish provided they are sharp and properly adjusted, and this is

perfectly achievable with a little practice and understanding. They perform best on hardwoods and work equally well on green and most seasoned timbers, whether these are cleft or sawn, almost round or even square in section. Material is prepared to approximately ⅛in (3mm) over the required finished diameter.

For handwork the wood is held vertically in a vice, and as the tool is rotated around it under gentle pressure it moves down, the required diameter emerging through the tool. If square seasoned wood is being rounded it is sawn to the oversize dimensions given – 1⅛ × 1⅛in/28 × 28mm for example, to produce 1in (25mm) in diameter in the round – and is first put through a larger diameter rounder which removes the correct amount of material off the corners, making it a snug fit in the appropriate size 1in (25mm) tool which is then used to finish off.

Under normal circumstances rounders shouldn't be removed once they are started; moreover do not work from opposite ends or a mismatch might occur. To complete the last portion of wood gripped in the vice, it must be repositioned so that the rounded part is held in the vice either horizontally or vertically, and the rounder rotated sideways or upwards and so off the end. If a rounding machine is used it is normally necessary to round by hand as above until there is sufficient wood through the rounder to be gripped in the machine chuck.

Where the machine method is followed, the prepared wood with the appropriate rounder still in place is held in the chuck; then with the machine slowly turning, the tool is held firmly against the torque and preferably against the wooden bedway for safety. It is then pushed gently along the revolving wood and off at the far end, thus producing a dowel of constant diameter. For tapering, the wood is first rounded to a parallel dowel, and is then gradually tapered using the trapping plane, the amount of taper governed by the amount of 'squeeze' given to the tool and the number of passes made.

Rounders are excellent for accurate jointing: tenon ends of rails and stretchers are quickly and precisely reduced to the required sizes, and in combination with drills of matching sizes, well-fitting round tenon and mortice joints are produced. Components turned on the conventional lathe or those made by drawknifing can be readily jointed in the same way. I often turn Windsor chair legs in their green, unseasoned state, leaving the joint area oversize and use a rounder to complete the joint tenon when dry.

(Opposite)
(Top left) Rounder being used to size joint of lathe-turned leg
(Top right) Rounder being used with rounding machine
(Below) Trapping plane in use on rounding machine

Seat Shaping

For shaping a chair seat, choose a method which suits you best, but in every case the seat blank should be securely held whilst it is being worked on. If using the adze, immobilise the seat between two substantial battens fixed to a board, then stand on the board. Swing the adze with care and allow the tool to 'follow through' – don't allow it to dig in – working generally across the grain. If the short-handled adze is used, the seat may be held vertically in the vice and the adze used with a downward chopping action. Again, work across the grain and let the tool follow through. Where a gouge and mallet is used – and this is quite a good, safe method – the seat should be held to the bench with 'G' cramps or a bench holdfast and the work started in the middle, working outwards. Do not get too deep too soon, but complete the work in two or three stages.

The inshave in use

The adze in use

These methods leave a rough surface in need of smoothing; failing a travisher, either a double-curved sole spokeshave or an inshave may be used. Both can be used across, with, or diagonally to the grain; and the wild grain of elm will require that you work in all these directions. Try to finish *with* the grain where possible, and as well as checking by eye, 'feel' the surface contours smooth with the fingertips. A scraper is used for final finishing; and a curved cabinet scraper with a positive hook will remove fine shavings (like butterflies' wings) and leave an almost burnished appearance. Use abrasive paper only if you must. For this stage the bench holdfast or 'G' cramps secure the workpiece to the bench.

The inshave can be more than just a smoothing tool: it can be used to hollow a seat from beginning to end, and in fact I often use it this way. Begin in the centre of the seat and work outwards, mainly across and diagonally to the grain. Work aggressively to begin with, twisting the wrists to give a scooping action and, like the adze, the follow-through which prevents the tool digging in. Finish off by taking finer cuts, and work right up to the outer mark which should be left as a crisp line to emphasise the seat shape. It may be considered a little tedious, but this method does have its advantages: the tool does not at any stage leave the rough surface that other methods do; it is kind to the wood; and furthermore, it is perfectly safe … and quiet.

The double hollow or saddle shape with central 'cod piece' is traditional, and its objective is comfort. It need not be too deep as long as the front edge is well rounded over, but deep saddling in fact gives a chair more character and I like to do it. The aim should be to remove approximately half the thickness of the seat at its deepest part, and then to keep that area fairly flat (see cross-sections in relevant diagrams in Part Two). Grain direction in the seat is always somewhat arbitrary and is usually decided by the width of the board. However, grain running fore and aft, back to front, is chosen whenever possible, not just for appearances' sake but because it means having to deal with end grain only once, at the back of the seat hollow, and not twice as when it occurs on each side.

Seat edges are chamfered with a spokeshave, the seat held vertically in a vice. The bottom edge chamfering is emphasised to help reduce the visual weight of a thick seat, with a much smaller chamfer to the top edge married into the well-rounded-over front edge. Look closely at old chairs to appreciate the subtlety of this shaping.

Remove all marks from the seat edge and from what remains level on the top surface; finish with a scraper. The underside should be roughly cleaned up; alternatively it can be planed smooth, but this only wastes time and wood and was rarely done in the past.

SEAT WEAVING

Seat weaving with rush – 'rushing' – was normally a separate craft, and for those wishing to do their own I recommend a good course or book (see page 151), followed by practice. Briefly, the rush must be made 'mellow' *ie* moist and pliable, by being soaked in water for several minutes, then drained and wrapped overnight in damp sacking or similar. As each rush is taken up for use it is squeezed with a cloth between finger and thumb from tip to butt to clean it and to remove excess air. Brittle tips are broken off.

Rushing begins by taking two or more squeezed rushes, placing them butt to tip and twisting them together to form a strong, neat coil of even thickness (see diagram). This is wound around and over the chair-frame, twisting as the work proceeds but only where it is visible; underneath the rush is not twisted.

One method of starting is to tie the ends of the rushes tightly together with thin string, then to tie them inside and midway along the left-hand seat-rail. They are then brought forwards towards the front rail and, smoothing and flattening with one hand and twisting with the other to make sufficient coil to go over the front rail, down in front and just below it. Twisting is always away from the nearest corner. The rush coil then goes below the front rail, up behind it on

Seat weaving with rush

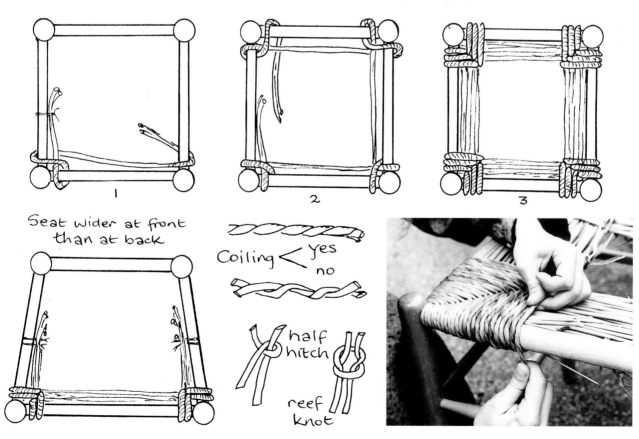

35

the inside of the chair frame and, smoothed and twisted again, goes to the left, over itself, and over and under the left-hand rail (see page 35). Then, without twisting, it goes across to the opposite side rail where, smoothed and twisted, it goes over the right-hand rail and down under it – and the process is repeated, continuously, at all four corners.

The rush coils must be even, pulled across the frame tightly and kept close together, while the cross-over which forms at the corners must be kept 'square'. New rushes must be joined on frequently, using reef or preferably half-hitch knots. These should never be tied where they will be seen, but underneath and tucked out of sight. Rush seats are padded using dry, waste rush or straw. Pockets which form at the corners are packed at intervals as the work proceeds. For seats wider across the front than the back there are methods for filling in the extra rail space; one is shown on page 35. The described sequence can then be followed.

The same methods may be used if weaving a seat with imported sea grass. This is already twisted and is worked dry, but the pattern sequence described above may be followed, omitting the damping and twisting.

BENDING

Several styles of country chair can be made without bent components, but sooner or later bending will be a required technique for many makers. Steam-bending equipment is described on pages 25 and 26. The technique is, arguably, the most difficult part of chairmaking and it is by no means an exact science; so don't worry if at first you have a few breakages – I, too, still have them.

Bends in wood can be fashioned by laminating techniques – and some chairmakers use this method – but it is not recommended; flexibility is lost because the several glue lines stiffen the components, formers need to be made much more precisely, and anyway, it isn't traditional!

Wood for solid bending must be straight-grained and free from knots and other defects. I once thought that unseasoned cleft wood was best for bending, but experience has shown that straight-grained sawn material of most tree species can be bent with equal success. And although green wood is physically the easiest to bend, the problems of distortion are greater since it is more likely to straighten out unless restrained, and drying times are longer than when wood has been allowed to dry at least partially before being bent. The stage at which the wood has lost the 'free water' from its cells (a moisture content of about

30 per cent) is about right, but air-dried wood dryer than this (MC 12 to 15 per cent) can be bent under favourable conditions. Kiln-dried wood is unsuitable for successful solid wood bending.

Wood is in the best condition for bending when it has been heated through at a maintained temperature of 100°C (boiling point of water) for approximately one hour per inch of thickness. Enclosure in a steam-box at atmospheric pressure is sufficient for this purpose – it heats and softens the fibres, rendering them more pliant and therefore less likely to fracture under the stresses and strains imposed by bending. It is the peculiarities of these stresses which can cause bending failure even in straight-grained wood. During bending, wood is subjected to two induced stresses: the fibres on the outside, or convex side are placed in tension, resulting in stretching, while those on the inside, or concave side, are in compression and so shortened. The first of these is the greater problem because heating increases the compressability of the fibres in greater proportion to the increase in their tensile (stretching) properties.

For extreme bends such as Windsor chair bows, the use of a supporting strap is a means of reducing the effect of this problem and of providing a mechanical aid to the bending process. In principle the strap itself restrains the convex surface of the wood, while the close-fitting end-stops reduce stretching virtually to nil. The back plates prevent any tendency for these to swivel under pressure, while the handles provide additional leverage which reduces the required physical effort. More elaborate bending straps have adjustable end-stops which can allow a small amount of stretching to combat excessive compression.

All steam-bending requires an organised approach and attitude, and preparation beforehand is important. Check that formers and supporting straps, where used, are ready and able to withstand the considerable

Steamed piece in position ready for bending

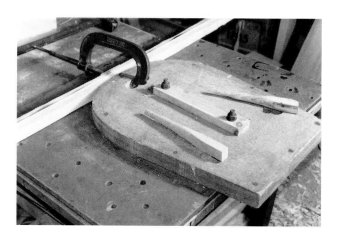

Bending the steamed piece into a bow

pressures involved, and that the steaming equipment is satisfactory. Have cramps, gloves, pegs and a mallet at the ready, and if possible, a competent and briefed assistant. Several pieces of wood can be steamed together, but ensure that those required first are accessible first.

Before placing in the steam-box, check that the wood for Windsor bows, bent with supporting straps, is of the correct length to fit properly between the straps' end-stops, and that both ends are cut square. Mark the centre point of the bend clearly, for quick location after steaming. In the steam-box, components should not be in contact with each other or the side of the box as this leads to uneven heating and can cause staining. Warm up the supporting straps on top of the steam-box. Windsor bow bends of 1¼ × 1¼in (32 × 32mm) section require a full hour's steaming.

No time should be lost when wood is taken out of the box, as loss of heat will cause problems. Wear gloves, and beware of hot steam on wrists and arms; remember that spectacles will mist up immediately. Where a supporting strap is used, quickly place the wood into it, place it onto the former, cramp at the centre point and pull the two halves, simultaneously if possible, around the former, keeping it in contact with the base board or bending table, all with a smooth, steady movement. Once fully round or nearly so, hold

Bending equipment and finished bows

it in place with pegs, then add a sash cramp if required. All this should take no more than a minute or two at the most.

The back uprights of ladderback and spindleback chairs are bent in matching pairs on the formers described in Fig 18 on page 75, where they are held in place with shaped blocks and cramps. Before going into the steam-box, each piece should be clearly marked so that they go quickly onto the former correctly, the bottom to the bottom stop. Uprights of 1½in (38mm) diameter require approximately 1¼ hours in the steam-box. Supporting straps are not normally required for these bends as the curvature is quite small, but quick

Sloping platform in use, drilling a chair seat

work when bending is essential and a hot, damp cloth placed on the area of greatest curvature during the bending process is a help. Note that wood is softened by steaming, and round surfaces can be flattened under pressure against hard flat surfaces.

Ladderback back-slats need only 15 minutes and *no more* in the steam-box; any longer, and they distort across their width. In the steam-box they should be separated by sticks placed between each one, though in the former several may be placed together and bent simultaneously. Curved back rails for spindlebacks can be in the steam-box for about 30 minutes, and are bent in formers similar to those used for ladderback slats.

Opinions vary about drying or setting times, and it all depends upon several interacting factors: the cross-section of the wood, its moisture content before bending, the workshop environment, and so on. Windsor bow bends, restrained in a wire binding, can be removed from the former within minutes of being bent but must be kept in the supporting strap for several days in a warm (65°F/18°C) place, or for a shorter period at a higher temperature. A rough

indication of readiness is given when the restraining wire feels loose. Back uprights, back-slats and back rails should be kept on their respective formers until dry and set – check the cramps until they feel loose. Do try not to be in a hurry, and allow bends time to set properly.

JOINTING

Country chair construction relies mainly on good, round tenon and mortice joints, that is, turned or otherwise shaped round tenons which fit snugly into round, bored mortices. Tenon making has already been described on page 32, and the corresponding mortices have to be consistently made at the correct size and at the proper angle if a chair is to 'sit' right. Some have to be at precisely 90°, many are at angles other than 90°; a lot are at compound angles into flat surfaces, others into components round in section. You can try doing this by hand and eye alone, or set a sliding bevel as a guide, or use a simple block guide. I have used all these methods, and the actual angle, give or take a degree or two, is not all that critical (honest!). But repeating it,

Sliding cradle in use and angle finder

and usually more than twice, can cause problems. Furthermore, drilling by hand into hard hardwood is physically difficult, and this tends to allow the drill to wander and the socket to become wrongly angled, or worse, oversize. So for all these reasons I now use and recommend for serious chairmaking in a workshop situation the use of a drilling machine and the simple jigs described on page 27.

A note on the drilling angles used in the projects which follow. Whilst recognising vertical, conventionally, as 90°, I find it easier to refer all other angles to zero degrees (0°) so that given-angles are equal on both sides and not plus or minus 90°. Example: 10° by this method means that number of degrees *either* side of vertical; less confusing than when it is either 80° or 100°.

The sloping platform is used mainly when drilling solid wood for the seats of stools and Windsor chairs, and is particularly useful when drilling at compound angles. It is used in conjunction with the alignment or sight-lines which have been calculated to provide the correct angle and are given in the individual projects in

Part Two. In practice, the sloping platform is fixed to the drill table, set to the prescribed angle, and the drill depth-stop correctly adjusted. Now the drill is lined up with the appropriate mark for drilling, and the sight-line drawn on the seat is aligned with the centre line of the sloping platform where it is firmly held by hand or by cramping, and the socket drilled to its prescribed depth. Following the same procedure and drilling each socket of a particular angle in turn ensures correctly angled sockets consistently.

The platform angle is measured by means of a protractor or an angle-finder, and is kept in position by a retaining block, as shown. Remember to reset the depth stop on the drill each time the angle is changed, and always start the drilling with care and not too much initial pressure otherwise the rim of the Forstner bit will skid. Once the bit has bitten, normal drilling pressure can be applied.

Drilling sockets into round components is simplified if they are held in a 'V' cradle (page 27); the simple one shown at (a) is adequate for most jobs. Ensure that multiple sockets are in line by aligning the drill with a short length of dowel in the first hole drilled. For second stage drilling, *ie* sockets at 90° (or other angles) to previously drilled sockets, use a short dowel and the angle-finder as shown to ensure accuracy. The same 'V' cradle is used to drill stretcher sockets into Windsor chair legs. In this case the cradle is set at a suitable angle, as shown in appropriate places in Part Two.

The more elaborate sliding 'V' cradle and cramps shown at (b) help considerably when drilling in-line sockets in the uprights of ladderback and spindleback chairs. For second-stage drilling, the procedure described above is followed. It is also useful when making the slot mortices for ladderback back-slats either by the chain-drilling method or when using the chairmaker's mortice bit. For use with the latter, the upright, held firmly in the sliding cradle, is moved sufficiently from side to side with one hand, whilst the other hand operates the drill's lever handle to progressively deepen the mortice to the extent of the depth stop. This operation should be started carefully and not rushed, the slot deepened in easy stages avoiding vibration so as not to overload and risk breaking the bit. Eye protection should be worn. The ends of the mortice slots are left round to suit the shape of the back-slats.

Drilling sockets for the back-sticks into the concave surface of Windsor back- or top-bows is done by eye. Socket positions are marked as described in the relevant projects in Part Two, and the bow placed

Drilling back bow sockets

'upsidedown' in a bench vice, front facing forward. Holes can be drilled by hand (a rachet brace is best), or with the aid of an adjustable-speed electric drill *on slow start* (this is important). The brace or drill is aligned with marked lines and angled slightly backward (3°–4°) to allow for the 'rake' of the back when drilling. A sliding bevel placed on the bench helps, or get someone to 'sight' for you. Central sockets are easy; outside sockets are started with the drill point at right-angles to the surface of the bow, then brought slowly to the correct drilling angle once the drill has bitten. Take care not to drill too deep.

Saw-toothed Forstner bits are recommended (page 27) for drilling joint sockets when these methods are followed; they produce the preferred parallel-sided, accurately sized, flat-bottomed sockets which complement the parallel tenons. For most chairs I use mainly blind joints, not through-joints. There are advocates of the through, wedged tenon for legs into seats and opinions that they make a better joint. Certainly they can make joints tight and are decorative when well done, but they make extra work, take care cleaning up, can protrude on the seat surface and are no longer necessary with good joints and modern adhesives.

Tapered, through, wedged joints are said to have the

A chairmaker's set of Forstner bits

added advantage of a 'friction bond', (like the engineers' Morse taper): that is, if the wood should shrink, the joint is 'relocked' each time someone sits on the chair (or so it is claimed). Apparently common on eighteenth-century American Windsors it sounds fine; making the tapered joint is not too difficult, and the tools are available; *but* again, it is extra work, etc, and requires more skill to get right.

Blind tapered joints have been suggested, while tapered tenons into parallel sockets is a trick guaranteed to make a joint go 'tight' at assembly – but its limited surface contact makes for an inferior joint. Gap-filling glues get recommended for such joints, and for loose-fitting ones, but this is a recipe for disaster. 'Fox wedging' is an old joinery idea (a kind of blind wedge technique). It needs experience to get the wedge size just right: too big and the tenon won't go in, too small and it was all a waste of time.

The parallel, blind socket of adequate depth, combined with a well-made, 'interference-fit' tenon provides maximum surface contact for gluing and, using dry wood, makes a perfectly satisfactory joint. Extra security may be given by pegging or wedging those joints which are in tension, or put into tension by handling, such as arm supports, back-bows and ladderback back-splats. Another advantage is that assembling chairs under 'tension' results in some joints being in compression, thus increasing pressure on joint surfaces and improving their hold; ladderback and spindleback chairs 'sprung' together under tension have their joints in compression; so do Windsor stretchers which are made long enough to push the legs apart, and some of this compression is transmitted to the leg joint into the seat; steam-bent back-bows and crinoline stretchers are similarly advantaged.

A resurgence of interest in 'green' woodworking has brought forth a good deal of debate on old ways of making chairs and on exploiting the property of shrinkage in wood to tighten joints. The principle here lies in the fact that round-section wood dries to an oval shape due to the differential between tangential and radial shrinkage. The theory is, that careful orientation of the growth-rings of dry round tenons into holes bored into wet uprights or legs, whose growth-rings have also been carefully orientated in the opposite plane, will produce tight joints as the wood dries out. The theory has been scientifically tested, and is used and advocated by some present-day green chairmakers.

I have no arguments against this theory, and 'ovalling', as it is known, is certainly found in the joints of some old chairs. But whether this is proof that the old chairmakers knew all about differential shrinkage and always assembled joints accordingly, or that those chairs which provide the 'evidence' were assembled that way by chance, is difficult to say. In any case, where horizontal rails or stretchers enter vertical legs or uprights in adjacent faces, growth-ring orientation can only be a compromise between what is theoretically correct and what is incorrect, anyway. I do not normally use the method, but prefer to rely on the proven advantages of assembling components only after they are all properly dry and stable, and therefore less likely to become victim to the central heating and drying system of most modern homes.

ASSEMBLY AND FINISHING

Final assembly of chairs is made easier if you ensure that all parts fit together individually, and then in unison with other parts. Check that all the components are the correct length for the chair you are making – some are purposely oversize initially to allow for differences and adjustments. Have a 'dry run' with the complete chair before gluing up. It helps if components can be marked for identification purposes before gluing begins, to avoid confusion and decision-making at a critical stage. Pencil marks on the ends of tenons are helpful. Components should be smoothed and cleaned up by scraping, and by using fine abrasive paper where necessary.

USE OF SANDING SEALER

A technique which I frequently use when a chair is to be clear finished by wax polishing is to apply a coat of sanding sealer to all components before assembly – it is much easier to do at this stage than after the chair is completed. However, care must be taken not to get sealer on to joint areas as this inhibits glue adhesion. Tenons may be covered by masking tape, although this isn't necessary if sealer application is controlled. Apply sealer with a brush or a cloth, but do not overload either. It dries extremely quickly, and should be gently sanded with a very fine abrasive or Scotsbright pad to flatten any raised grain. Wipe away the white powder residue.

FRICTION POLISHING

A further technique where seasoned wood is turned in a power lathe is that of friction polishing, in which sealer and wax or a proprietary polish is applied on a cloth to a component while it is revolving in the lathe.

This is an approved woodturner's method, and wood can be brought to a high polish by this method. However, great care should be taken not to get trailing ends of cloth caught up in the lathe or the component.

GLUING-UP

Final gluing-up and assembly should be an organised procedure, done in the correct sequence given in Part Two. The use of a 'protected bench' is advocated: a bench or sturdy table covered with an old piece of clean blanket or carpet, or even corrugated packing, to protect the chair from marking on a hard surface. Have glue and a damp cloth at the ready, and a soft mallet to encourage tight joints to fit. Cramps are hardly ever required if joints are tight-fitting, though a cramp *is* sometimes helpful to push tight joints together. Assemble as described for individual chairs.

Old chairs were, of course, glued with the only one available, animal (or Scotch) glue; this can still be bought in granular form. It has to be heated in water, and used hot and very quickly. Its advantage is that it can be remelted, and this is a boon to furniture restorers. Of the many modern adhesives, those based upon PVA are the most commonly used today, and are the most suitable; their slight elasticity gives some advantage over other glues which are more brittle, and they are convenient in use.

FINAL FINISHING

Final finishing may be carried out according to choice. Some chairmakers apply no finish at all, as was traditional with very early country chairs, but a finish of some kind is advisable as a protection as well as for the sake of appearance. Where sealer was applied, or friction-polishing carried out earlier, the chair is best finished clear, as intended, by wax polishing. Use a good quality beeswax and turpentine polish and apply this with a cloth two or three times; buff between each application, finally polishing with a soft cloth. Alternatively, an oil finish may be given. This is applied with a cloth, and after a period of drying any surface surplus is wiped off.

Some wood stains can be applied after using sanding sealer, but if a stain is to penetrate it should be used before the sealer is applied. I stain very few of the chairs I make because I prefer the natural waxed finish. However, sometimes staining or colouring *is* required, and three of the chairs described in Part Two are stained: the spindleback (page 120) was given a light oak water-stain, mainly to give the chair an antique finish and to enhance the grain. After staining and when thoroughly dry, the surface was lightly sanded then sealed, and sanded again, and finally wax polished. The Gimson ladderback (page 114) and the double bow Windsor (page 136) were treated with potassium bichromate crystals dissolved in warm water, to darken the wood. After one application surfaces were sanded smooth when dry, and the chairs were given a second application. This was not sanded, but when it was dry, the chairs were then given a coat of sanding sealer and lightly sanded smooth. Both chairs were finally polished with two applications of dark (antique) wax polish. Proprietary brand wood-dyes could have been used instead of the chemical water-stain mix.

If a painted finish is required any good quality gloss paint may be used after suitable priming. Alternatively, the traditional paint known as milk paint (it contains casein) is very suitable. It dries to a matt finish but can be buffed to a dull gloss by wax polishing.

PART TWO

THE PROJECTS

STOOLS
BACKSTOOL
CHILD'S RUSH-SEAT CHAIR
COMB-BACK
SINGLE LADDERBACK
LOW BOW-BACK
CLISSETT LADDERBACK
SINGLE BOW WINDSOR
ROCKING CHAIR
GIMSON LADDERBACK
SPINDLEBACK
SMOKER'S BOW
DOUBLE BOW WINDSOR

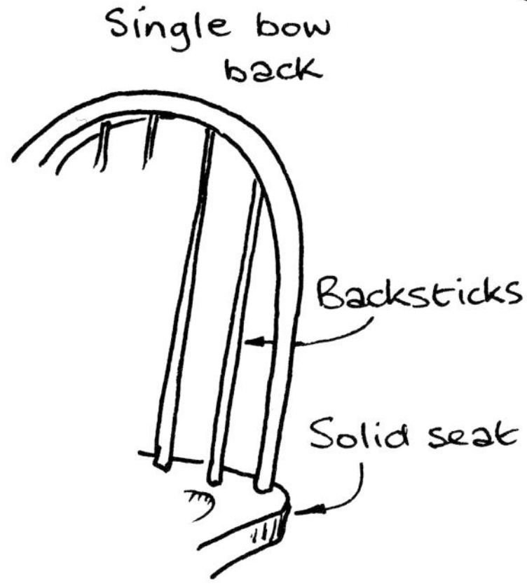

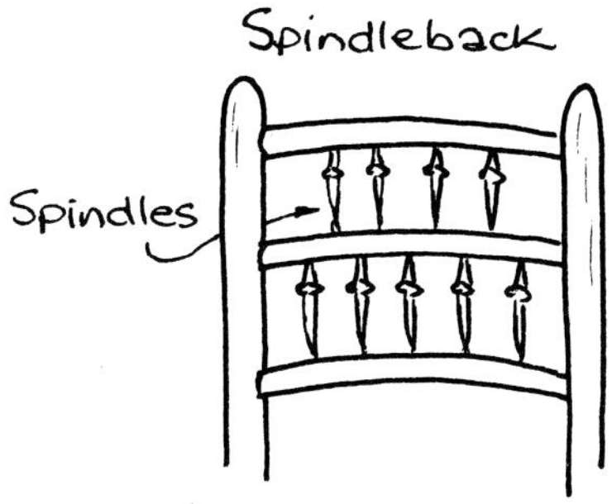

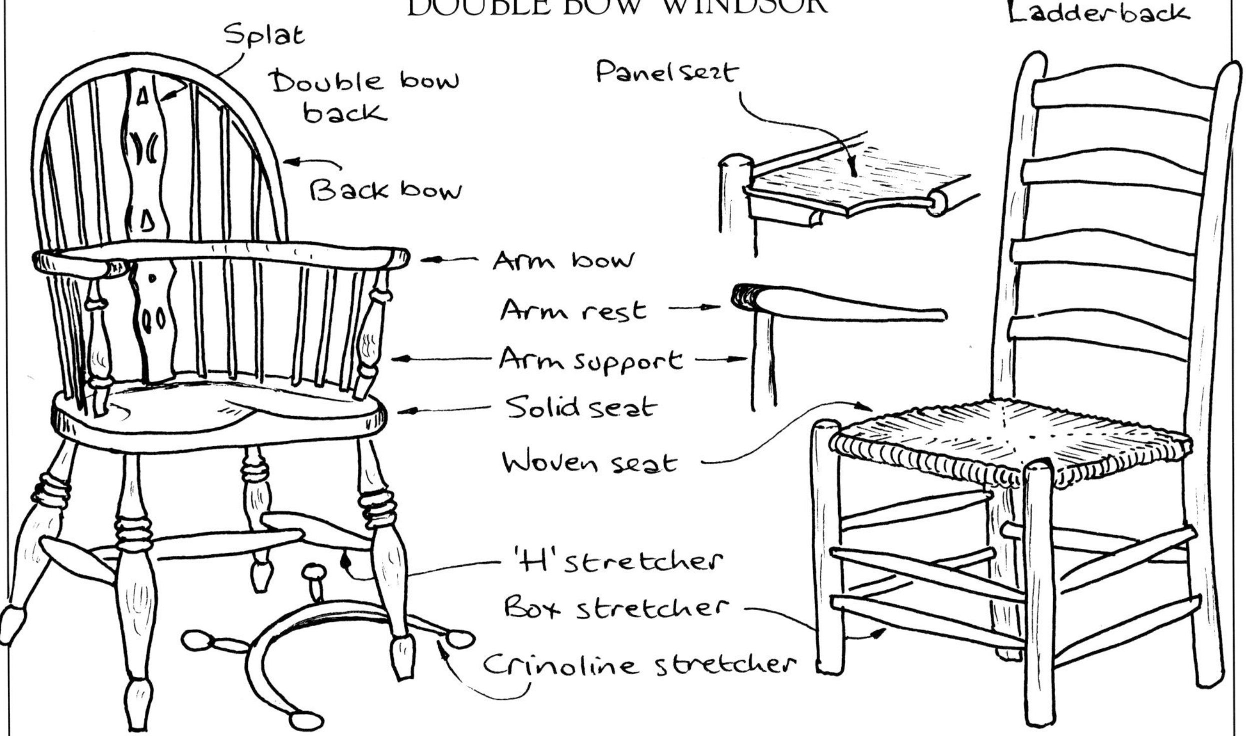

Comb back

Single bow back

Backsticks

Solid seat

Spindleback

Spindles

Splat

Double bow back

Back bow

Panel seat

Ladderback

Arm bow

Arm rest

Arm support

Solid seat

Woven seat

'H' stretcher

Box stretcher

Crinoline stretcher

STOOLS

Most books on furniture history would have us believe that early stools were either of the trestle type, or were the heavy, 'joyned' sort of stool dating back to medieval times. With their mortice-and-tenon jointed rails and thick plank top they were the product of the joiner's workshop: hence the latter's name.

Alongside these, however, there were two other types of stool in use, found in the cottages of the poorer classes, in farmhouse kitchens, and 'below stairs' in the servants' quarters of the gentry. The work of village carpenters and turners, the first of these was a simple, solid-top stool consisting of a thick wooden seat, round or rectangular, into which were socketed three or sometimes four plain legs which might be either turned or shaped by hand. At first, leg joints were drilled through and secured by wedging; later, stopped or 'blind' joints became more common. The legs themselves were splayed outwards for stability, the popular three-legged stools, legs spread tripod fashion, being best able to cope with the often uneven floors of

early dwellings. The so-called milking stool is a typical early, low, three-legged example; while the inclusion here of a tall, four-legged version is to illustrate the sort that, later, was used widely in workplace, home and hostelry.

The other kind of stool was made quite differently, being of an open frame construction and having a woven seat. Basically it consisted of four plain turned legs, into which were socketed, at right-angles, four top rails at seat level and four more below to act as stretchers; the seat was woven, most often with rushes, sometimes with willow. This type of stool would clearly have provided a higher level of comfort than the solid-seated variety, and proved to be very popular in many regions.

These two 'country' style stools form the basis of the many styles of country chair and are worthy of a place here at the start, not only for their own sakes but as useful prototypes from which can be learned many of the basic skills required later.

Two old cottage stools

SOLID-SEAT STOOLS

SEAT SHAPING AND MARKING-OUT

1 Cut seat to size, preferably circular if the three-legged version is being made, circular or rectangular if it is to have four legs.

2 Smooth off both flat surfaces and choose best side for top of stool. Clean up edges, rounding or chamfering off for added comfort.

3 If making with wedged 'through'-joints, mark out on top surface for drilling; if making with 'blind' joints, mark out on underside (Fig 1).

4 Mark out for three or four legs as shown.

SEAT DRILLING

5 Drill angled leg sockets in seat as appropriate, using sloping platform set to correct angle of 20°, making use of alignment lines (see page 38). Or drill by other means, 1in (25mm) diameter.

6 If drilling 'through'-holes, remember to drill from the top. If drilling 'blind' holes, remember to set depth-stop on drilling machine or arrange some other method of depth control, and drill from underneath. (See note about depth of drilled sockets, page 47.)

SHAPING AND CHECKING LEGS

7 Prepare wood for legs by sawing or cleaving. Turn to size, or shape by hand, or use rounders.

8 Form top joint, 1in (25mm) diameter, and 1¼in (32mm) long if for 'blind' joint, 1¾in (44mm) for 'through'-joint. Turn or whittle to size, or use a 1in (25mm) rotary plane.

9 Try legs for fit in seat sockets. For four-legged stools, check on level surface that leg lengths are even, otherwise stool will rock (with three-legged stools this problem does not arise). Correct if necessary.

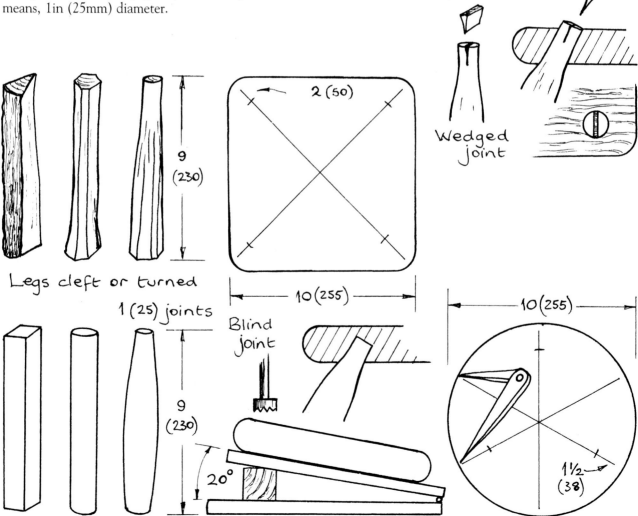

FIG. 1

Wedged joint

Legs cleft or turned

1 (25) joints

Blind joint

2 (50)

10 (255)

9 (230)

9 (230)

10 (255)

20°

1½ (38)

Wedging through-joints in the stool

WEDGED 'THROUGH'-JOINTS

10 Legs for these joints will require a saw cut in joint end to accommodate wedges, and wedges to be made. Saw cut should be central and approximately 1in (25mm) down leg joint. Make hardwood wedges by sawing as shown, and trim to size (Fig 1).

NOTE: When wedges are fitted during assembly it is important that they lie at right angles to grain of seat. Otherwise, the force of wedge will split seat along grain. Done correctly, wedge tightens leg securely into seat socket.

'BLIND' JOINTS

11 These are not drilled through. Leg tenons must be a good tight fit and go down to full depth of socket.

NOTE: Drilled socket depths for legs should always be at least equal to tenon diameter and preferably deeper, *eg* tenon diameter 1in (25mm), socket depth 1⅛in (28mm) or 1¼in (32mm) if possible. Joints should be an 'interference fit'; do not rely on gap-filling glues.

Cleaning off after wedging

47

ASSEMBLY

12 Clean off all surfaces, and sand to a fine finish. Check that joint areas are clean and dust-free.

13 With seat upside-down on a clean, flat, protected surface on bench, put sufficient glue into socket holes. Do not use too much glue, and ensure that it is spread around on sides of socket and not just lying on bottom where it will serve little purpose.

14 For 'through' wedged joints, insert legs until they protrude through seat, aligning each one so that their wedges will lie across grain of seat. Stand stool upright on bench top and tap all wedges part way in, then tap each one again until they are all tightly home. A hammer is actually better for this job than a mallet.

15 Check stability of stool, wipe off surplus glue and leave to dry. When dry, saw off stub ends almost flush with stool top, taking care not to damage surface. Clean off flush with a sharp chisel or a block plane, and finish with a cabinet scraper or fine abrasive paper.

16 For 'blind' joints, keep seat upside-down on protected surface, insert legs, and tap home to their full depth. Check for stability. Wipe off any surplus glue and leave to dry.

FINISHING

17 Clean off all surfaces and apply a coat of sanding sealer. Rub this down with fine abrasive paper and finish off with wax polish (see notes in Assembly and Finishing, pages 41 and 42, on suggested method of applying sealer before assembly).

Round stool parts

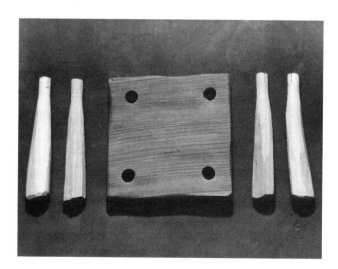

Square stool parts

SQUARE STOOL		CUTTING LIST (Add waste)	
No.	ITEM	INCHES	mm
4	Legs	9 × 1½ × 1½	230 × 38 × 38
1	Seat	10 × 10 × 1¾	255 × 255 × 44
ROUND STOOL			
No.	ITEM	INCHES	mm
3	Legs	9 × 1½ × 1½	230 × 38 × 38
1	Seat	10 × 10 × 1¾	255 × 255 × 44

TALL STOOL

SEAT SHAPING AND MARKING OUT

1 Cut seat to size. Use hand-saw or bandsaw.

2 Clean up flat surfaces and edges. Choose best surface as top.

3 Mark out for four leg sockets as shown (Fig 2).

SEAT DRILLING

4 Drill angled leg sockets using pillar drill and sloping platform set at correct angle of 12° and using alignment lines. Follow previous instructions for either 'through' or 'blind' holes (pages 46 and 47).

5 Note that drilling angle is less than for lower stool; this reduces excessive splay of legs in tall stools.

SHAPING LEGS

6 Prepare wood for legs. Turn to size, or shape by hand if plain legs are preferred.

7 Form the top joints, 1in (25mm) diameter and 1¼in (32mm) long if 'blind' joints, 1¾in (44mm) long if 'through'-joints. Turn or whittle to size, or use a 1in (25mm) rotary plane (Fig 2).

8 Try legs for fit; they should be tight. Check they go all the way into sockets. Stand on level surface and check for uneven leg lengths which will cause stool to rock. Correct if necessary.

SHAPING STRETCHERS

9 Make four stretchers as shown. The length dimensions given may prove generous and some adjustment may have to be made later (see note below). Form ⅞in (22mm) joints at each end, but do not shoulder them.

NOTE: The inclusion of this type of stool at this stage is to give experience of making and fitting stretchers, an important structural element in most country chairs. Normally, stools and chairs with legs exceeding 12in (305mm) in length require stretchers to strengthen the construction. When in position stretchers should, literally, stretch the legs apart so they are fully efficient, therefore their finished length should permit this.

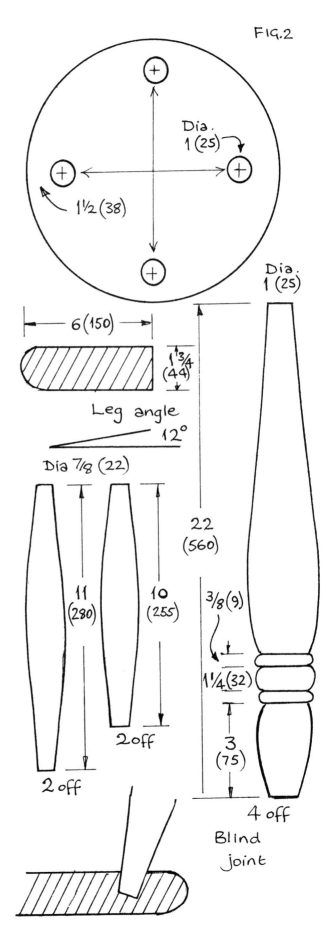

FIG.2

Dia. 1 (25)

1½ (38)

6 (150)

1¾ (44)

Leg angle 12°

Dia ⅞ (22)

Dia. 1 (25)

22 (560)

11 (280)

10 (255)

3/8 (9)

1¼ (32)

3 (75)

2off

2 off

4 off

Blind Joint

MARKING STRETCHER SOCKETS IN LEGS (I)

10 Sockets for stretchers lie at right-angles (90°) to each other (Fig 3). Marking out and drilling as described eliminates potential problems with this stage.

11 Treat legs as two separate pairs initially and join these together to form two single-rung 'ladders' (Fig 3).

12 Begin by drawing centre lines on each leg and on these, measuring from the top, mark drilling centres for stretcher sockets at 12in (305mm). Mark only one centre on each leg for now.

DRILLING LEGS (I)

13 Because the stool legs are splayed (angled outwards) the stretcher sockets must also be drilled at an angle.

14 Using the 'V' cradle described on page 27, set at the correct angle, 7°, drill each leg at the marked place, ⅞in (22mm) dia, ⅞in (22mm) deep (Fig 3).

NOTE: Due to the nature of the compound angle of the legs, the stretcher angle is always less than the leg angle. For reference purposes, when drilling legs for stretchers, the top *ie* the joint end of the leg, should be at the highest point.

FIRST TRIAL PARTIAL ASSEMBLY

15 Check that stretchers (the shortest two) fit correctly and to full depth in individual legs.

16 With seat upside-down on flat surface, insert all four legs part-way into seat sockets and manipulate the two shortest stretchers into place. Push stretchers in and push legs down simultaneously, both to full depth. If this proves excessively difficult or impossible, reduce the length of both stretchers slightly and try again.

17 When satisfactory, leave partially assembled.

MARKING STRETCHER SOCKETS IN LEGS (II)

18 With legs in place, mark position of drilling centres for second set of stretcher sockets. These lie 2in

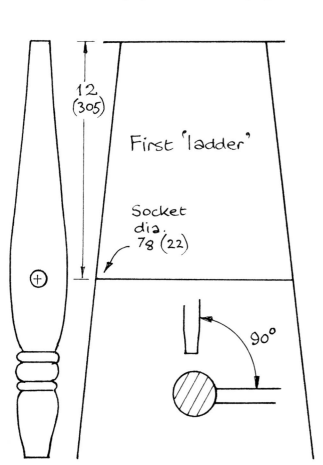

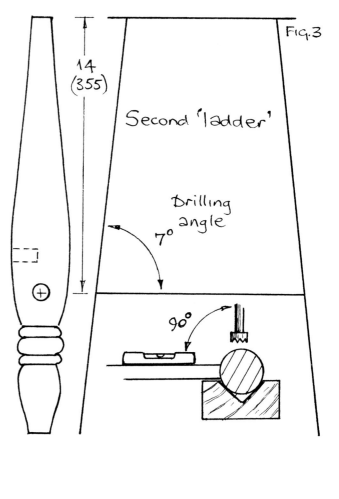

(50mm) below and at 90° around from sockets already drilled (Fig 3). This 'stagger' of the joints helps preserve the strength of the legs.

19 Make sure that the marked positions face inwards and towards each other. Mark with a clear pencil line. Disassemble.

DRILLING LEGS (II)

20 This second drilling must produce sockets at right-angles (90°) to those previously drilled. Place each leg in turn in the 'V' cradle set at the same correct angle (7°) and insert a short length of ¾in (19mm) dowel into the previously drilled hole. Using a spirit level, set this to lie horizontally, then drill vertically into the leg at the marked position (Fig 3).

TRIAL FULL ASSEMBLY

21 With seat on a flat surface, insert all four legs part-way into seat sockets, manipulate first the short stretchers, then the longer ones into place, and push or tap legs down almost to full depth. Adjust stretcher lengths if this is still necessary, and try again.

22 When satisfied, identify components and disassemble.

NOTE: If components go together too tightly and legs go to full depth it may be difficult to separate trial assembly. So beware: the difference between having a too-tight assembly and a too-loose assembly is quite subtle.

FINAL ASSEMBLY

23 Clean off all unnecessary marks. Check that joint

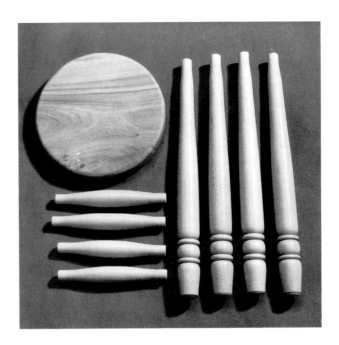

Tall stool parts

areas are clean and free from dust. Apply a coat of sanding sealer, if desired and rub down.

24 With seat upside-down on a clean, flat, soft surface, put glue in seat sockets and then in stretcher sockets, put legs part-way in, manipulate stretchers into place as previously, and press or tap all components home to their full depth.

25 Stand upright on a level surface and check for stability. Clean off any surplus glue and leave to dry.

FINISHING

26 Clean off any marks. If previously sealed and sanded, simply apply wax polish. Otherwise apply sealer, rub down and then apply wax polish.

TALL STOOL		CUTTING LIST (Add waste)	
No.	ITEM	INCHES	mm
4	Legs	22 × 2 × 2	560 × 50 × 50
4	Stretchers	11 × 1½ × 1½	280 × 38 × 38
1	Seat	12 × 12 × 1¾	305 × 305 × 44

WOVEN SEAT STOOL

MAKING LEGS AND RAILS

1 Prepare all material either by sawing or cleaving. Turn to size, or shape by hand, or use rotary planes.

2 Begin by making the four legs, 1⅜in (35mm) or 1½in (38mm) diameter, 12in (305mm) long. Then make eight rails, 1in (25mm) diameter. These, too, are all 12in (305mm) long (which is why I often call this a one foot stool!)

3 Both ends of the four legs should be chamfered or rounded off and the top ends sanded up smooth. Each end of the eight rails is reduced to ¾in (19mm) to form a joint. Note, these are not shouldered. The four rails which will be the lower (stretcher) rails may be given a tapered shape but this is not necessary for the top (seat) rails. Nor do these last four need to be smooth.

NOTE: Traditionally, seat rails were not round but of a flat oval section, only the ends being rounded to form the joints. They were cleft and shaped with the drawknife and left quite rough from the tool. This method produced a strong rail and the rough surface better for seat-weaving. For the beginner making this stool it is easier to do round rails, and these are quite adequate. The traditional method is described in detail on page 74.

FIRST MARKING OUT

4 Marking out rail sockets in the legs is made less complicated if, initially, two ends (or two sides) only are marked out and temporarily assembled. This eliminates potential problems with the right-angle (90°) drilling required (Fig 4). Treat legs as two separate pairs to begin with and join these together to make two very short 'ladders'.

5 Begin by drawing a centre line down each leg and, measuring from the top, mark on these drilling centres for the two rails at 1in (25mm) and again 6in (150mm) below this (Fig 5).

FIRST DRILLING

6 Using the 'V' cradle to support each leg in turn, drill this first set of sockets, ¾in (19mm) dia, ⅞in (22mm) deep. Make sure that pairs of sockets are 'in line' in leg: check by aligning drill with a short length of ¾in (19mm) dowel inserted into first hole drilled. Alternatively use the sliding 'V' cradle shown on page 27.

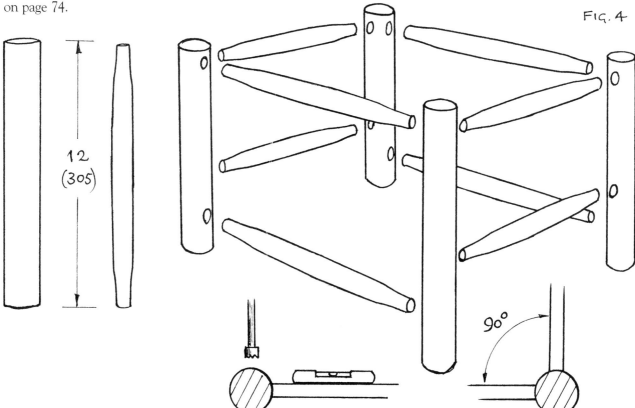

FIG. 4

12
(305)

90°

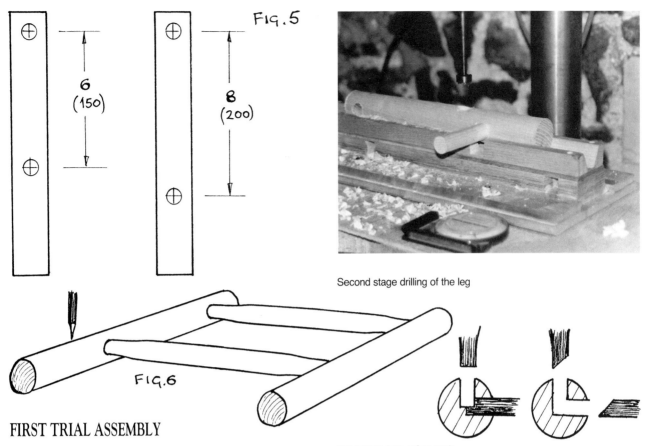

FIG.5

6
(150)

8
(200)

FIG.6

Second stage drilling of the leg

FIRST TRIAL ASSEMBLY

7 Check seat and stretcher rails for fit into sockets in each pair of legs; adjust if necessary and fit to full depth. Lay on flat surface and check for 'wind'. Correct by careful twisting if required.

SECOND MARKING OUT

8 With two ends (or sides) assembled and still flat on bench, mark position of second set of rail sockets. Measuring from top of each leg, mark centres at 1in (25mm) as before, but this time 8in (200mm) below this (Fig 5). This 'stagger' of the lower joints helps preserve the strength of the leg.

SECOND DRILLING

9 For this second stage of drilling, the assembled 'ladders' may be kept together and the final sockets drilled vertically from above to give the required 90° angle.

10 Alternatively, separate the parts, place each leg individually in the 'V' cradle and insert a short length of ¾in (19mm) dowel in one of the previously drilled holes. With a spirit level, set this to lie horizontally and drill vertically into the leg at the marked position (Fig 4).

SEAT RAIL JOINTS

11 It will be found that because the seat-rail joints are level (and not staggered), they break into each other (Fig 6). If stage 9 is followed this second drilling will remove part of the intruding tenon and permit final assembly if stretchers are replaced in exactly the same way. Identify with pencil marks to aid this. If stage 10 is followed it will be necessary to mitre the end of each tenon before final assembly (Fig 6).

Detail of top joint area

First stage assembly; two short 'ladders'

SECOND TRIAL ASSEMBLY

12 Check that all seat and stretcher rails are of equal length and fit individually into drilled sockets to full depth.

13 Begin by assembling first pair of ladders as before, correctly align ends of joint tenons.

14 Add additional rails to make complete stool frame: check they go to full depth. Stand on level surface to check for stability, and adjust if required by careful twisting. When satisfied, disassemble.

FINAL ASSEMBLY

15 Clean off all unnecessary marks; smooth legs and stretchers. Check that joint areas are clean and dust-free. If giving components a coat of sealer, do this now. There is no need to seal seat-rails.

16 Assemble first pairs of ladders. Put sufficient glue into sockets and spread around on sides of sockets; do

not leave lying on bottom where it will serve little purpose. Insert rails to full depth. Remember to align seat-rails correctly.

17 Put glue into remaining sockets in same way. Insert rails to full depth by tapping or pressing together.

18 Stand on level surface and check stool stands correctly. Wipe off any surplus glue and leave to dry.

NOTE: All joints should be pushed fully home by hand pressure or by gentle tapping with a soft mallet (one with a hide or plastic composition head.) Alternatively use a wooden mallet and a round-edged softwood block. Cramping should rarely be required, except perhaps to squeeze a stubborn stool or chair frame together. Keeping cramps in position whilst glue dries is normally unnecessary; joints should be tight enough not to require this.

FINISHING

19 Final finishing and polishing is left until after the stool frame has had its seat woven. If rush is used it is

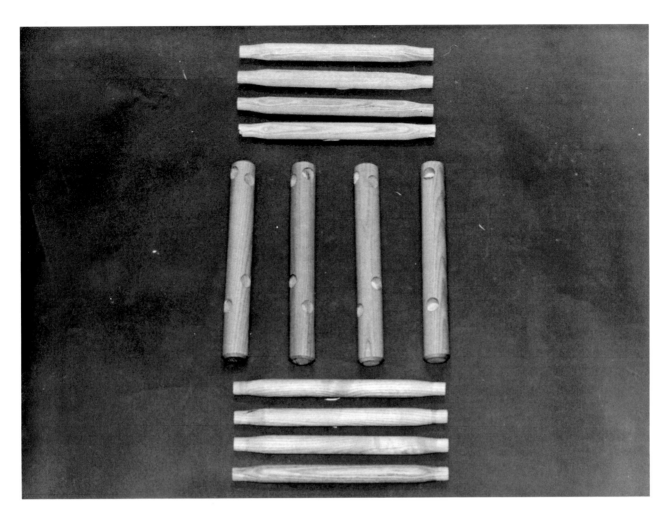

worked damp and this would spoil any finish given previously.

20 After the seat weaving is completed (see page 35) the frame can be sealed (if not done before), rubbed

Woven stool parts

down and then polished with a wax polish. Avoid getting sealer and wax polish on the woven seat material.

WOVEN SEAT STOOL CUTTING LIST (Add waste)			
No.	ITEM	INCHES	mm
4	Legs	12× 1½ × 1½	305 × 38 × 38
8	Rails	12 × 1 × 1	305 × 25 × 25

BACKSTOOL

Stools of various kinds, along with benches and settles, were the normal form of seating, particularly for the poorer classes, up until the reign of Elizabeth I. Hitherto only the master of the house and persons of high rank and status would have had, and been expected to use a chair: this would have been an armchair, high-backed and architectural in construction and commanding authority and respect, such a reputation giving rise to the term 'chairman' or its modern euphemism, 'chairperson'.

In due course, probably around the start of the seventeenth century, some stools were given backs as an aid to comfort, thus creating what came to be known as side or single chairs *ie* chairs without arms. At first they were not called chairs at all in order to preserve the dignity and status of the 'proper' chairs as used by chairpersons, but were known as 'backstools'

(a stool with a back) and occasionally as 'backchaires', according to an inventory of 1620.

The backstool described here is a logical development from the low, solid-seat stools included in the previous chapter. By the simple addition of short vertical back-sticks and a horizontal rail or bar, the transition is easily achieved; and perhaps most importantly, this development shows how its construction in turn gave rise to the so-called Windsor chair. Examples of this early type of backstool are to be found all over Britain, particularly in the Celtic regions.

The seat is a plain piece of elm board with three cleft legs of ash socketed and wedge-jointed into it; the back is of ash sticks, with a slightly shaped top rail or comb of elm. The backstool shown here was given an oil finish.

Early Welsh backstool

RECIPE

MAKING SEAT

1 Select a piece of elm and saw to the dimensions given in Fig 7. Smooth top of both surfaces, and clean up and chamfer edges.

2 Mark out position of leg sockets on top surface of seat (legs have through joints). Draw in alignment or sight lines as shown.

3 Drill the three holes 1⅜in (35mm) in diameter and through seat, all at 20° angle.

4 Mark out position of back-stick sockets on top surface of seat. Draw in alignment or sight lines if required, although these are not needed in this example as the drilling angle is not a compound angle.

5 Drill the four holes, 1in (25mm) diameter, 1¼in (32mm) deep, all at 8° angle.

MAKING LEGS

6 Select three pieces of ash, preferably cleft and ideally from the same tree as shown. Sawn timber can be used if necessary.

7 Shape as shown by drawknifing or work with spokeshave. Keep top joint area a little oversize initially, especially if wood is not fully dry.

MAKING BACK-STICKS AND COMB

8 Use cleft or sawn ash and make four sticks to sizes shown using lathe or rounders, or they can be shaped by drawknife or spokeshave. Joints should be 1in (25mm) diameter at bottom, ½in (12mm) diameter at top.

9 Saw out the curved top rail or comb and clean up surfaces.

10 Mark out underside edge as shown and drill the four holes, ½in (12mm) diameter, 1in (25mm) deep.

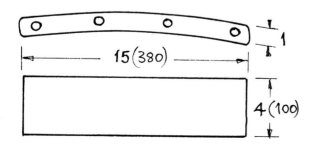

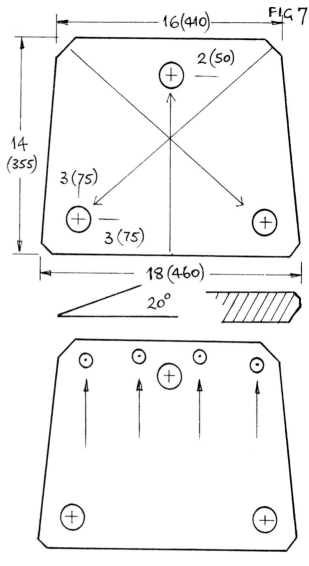

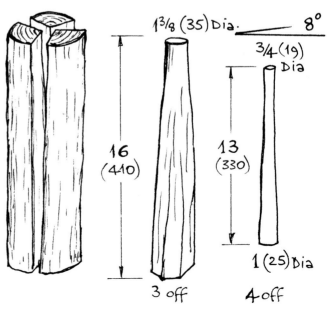

WEDGES FOR LEGS

11 Fit legs (without glue) and orientate to best position; they should protrude slightly above seat surface. Mark sawing line of slot for wedge at top of each leg (see page 46): line should lie across (at right angles to) grain of seat. Mark legs for identification purposes at assembly.

12 Remove legs and make saw-cut, about 1in (25mm) deep. Make wedges as previously shown.

PREPARATION FOR ASSEMBLY

13 Clean up all components. Smooth seat surface and comb but leave legs as finished with drawknife or spokeshave.

14 Trial-assemble (without glue) back-sticks into seat and add comb. Make any necessary adjustments and disassemble.

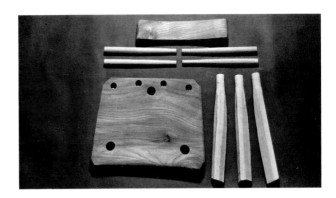

Backstool parts

Cleft legs glued and wedged

FINAL ASSEMBLY

15 Put glue into seat sockets, and insert legs respectively; check that each leg protrudes slightly and that wedge slot is correctly orientated. Stand on a solid surface and tap in wedges. Check again, and hammer wedges in tight. Clean off surplus glue. Cut off stub ends later when glue has dried.

16 Put glue into back-stick sockets in seat, insert back-sticks; put glue into sockets in comb and add comb. Push or tap down with soft mallet until joints are well home and comb is level. Clean off any surplus glue and leave until dry.

Final assembly of backstool

FINISHING

17 The chair illustrated was finished by oiling; I used tung oil, but others could be used. Alternatively the finish could be sanding sealer followed by wax polishing. See page 41 for advice.

BACKSTOOL CUTTING LIST (Add waste)			
No.	ITEM	INCHES	mm
1	Seat	16 × 14 × 1¾	410 × 355 × 44
3	Legs	16 × 2 × 2	410 × 50 × 50
4	Back-sticks	13 × 1 × 1	330 × 25 × 25
1	Comb	15 × 4 × 2	380 × 100 × 50

CHILD'S RUSH-SEAT CHAIR

This small chair is based on a chair said to have been used in early childhood by John Bunyan, the English preacher and writer, famous for his allegory, *The Pilgrims' Progress*. John Bunyan was born in 1628, which would date the original chair as early seventeenth century. Its relationship to and development from the woven-seat stool is self-evident, the upward extension of the pair of back legs forming the simple backrest and similarly at the front providing support for armrests. The three plain spindles in the backrest add a decorative touch and furnish strong 'country' links with the earlier, much more ornate Derbyshire chairs, and the later Midlands and northern counties spindle-back varieties which were so prolific.

The chair introduces the simple construction which was to account for the widespread production and use of chairs of this type. The adult-sized rush-seated ladderback is a further variant of this kind of construction (see later). In each case, the plain turned or otherwise shaped parts, and the round tenon joints were readily adopted by the village wheelwrights and carpenters, who would have produced many such chairs before chairmaking became a separate, specialised trade.

This child-size chair is made entirely in ash, although beech could be substituted. Instructions are given for making it as a rocking chair, but it could also be made as a plain chair without rockers; in this case an extra pair of side-rails would need to be added, and directions are given for anyone wishing to make this change.

Eighteenth century child's chair

RECIPE

MAKING MAIN UPRIGHTS

1 Prepare all material. Turn or shape by hand or use rotary planes (rounders).

2 Make two back uprights, 1½in (38mm) in diameter, 25in (635mm) long. Round and smooth over top ends.

3 Make two front uprights, 1½in (38mm) diameter, 16in (410mm) long. Round and smooth over top ends.

4 For the rocking chair, bottom ends of all four uprights are reduced to 1in (25mm) diameter to form joints into rockers.

MAKING CROSS-RAILS

5 Prepare all material. Turn or shape as above.

6 Make ten identical rails, each 1in (25mm) diameter, 12in (305mm) long (make twelve if not making the rocking chair).

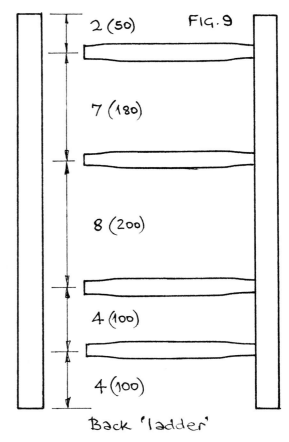

Back 'ladder'

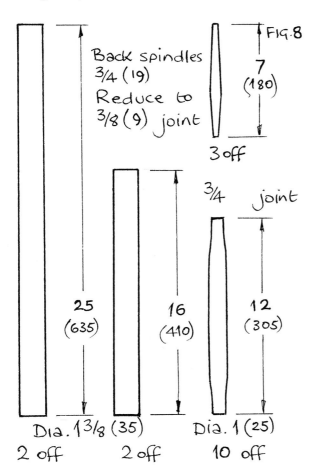

7 Each end of each rail is reduced to ¾in (19mm) to form joint tenons. The four seat-rails need not be smooth-finished.

MAKING BACK SPINDLES

8 Prepare material. Turn or shape as above.

9 Make three spindles, each one ¾in (19mm) diameter, 7in (180mm) long tapered at each end to ⅜in (9mm).

MARKING OUT FOR DRILLING

10 Marking out for rail sockets in uprights is simplified if, initially, the chair is regarded as two separate parts, a back and a front, each with side-to-side cross-rails which are later joined together by side-rails.

11 Begin by orientating uprights so that best grain figure faces forward. Then, on what will be the 'inside' face of each upright, draw a centre line and on this, on each upright, mark position of sockets for cross-rails. Refer to Fig 9 and Fig 10.

12 Mark only those centres for side-to-side cross-rails.

NOTE: This method of marking out and making first a back and then a front 'ladder', then joining these

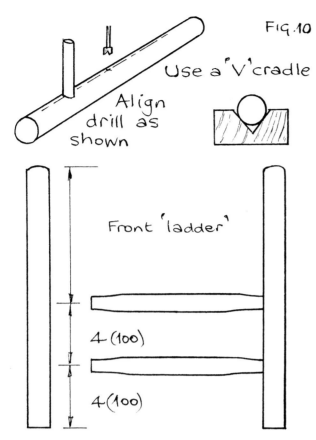

FIG. 10

Use a 'V' cradle

Align drill as shown

Front 'ladder'

4 (100)

4 (100)

together with side-rails (as advocated in the stool construction details given earlier), eliminates potential problems associated with the right-angle and splayed-angle drilling of adjacent sockets which is a feature of chair-frame construction. This possible problem and this same method of overcoming it recurs in other chairs of similar construction described later.

FIRST DRILLING

13 Using the 'V' cradle, drill each upright, vertically and at the marked positions, all at ¾in (19mm) diameter, ⅞in (22mm) deep.

14 Ensure that drilled sockets are in line with each other by aligning drill with a short length of ¾in (19mm) dowel in first hole drilled. Or use the sliding 'V'-cradle described on page 27.

FIRST TRIAL ASSEMBLY

15 Check that individual rails fit their sockets and go to full depth.

16 Then join pairs of uprights to make a back 'ladder' and a front 'ladder'.

17 Place on a flat surface and check for wind. Twist carefully to correct if necessary.

MARKING OUT FOR SECOND DRILLING

18 With back ladder still assembled on a flat surface, mark position of side-rail sockets on upper surface of each upright.

19 Repeat with front ladder, remembering to mark back-facing surface this time. Refer to Fig 11.

20 (Mark in extra, lower rail sockets only if not making the rocking chair.)

SECOND DRILLING

21 Either, keep ladders together and drill side-rail sockets vertically to give the necessary 90° angle.

22 Or, disassemble the ladders and, using the 'V' cradle, drill uprights separately. Insert a ¾in (19mm) dowel into a previously drilled hole and use a spirit level to set this horizontally. Drill vertically at the marked positions.

23 Keep sockets in line as described above (stage 14).

NOTE: Seat-rail joints have a slight overlap and will break into each other. If stage 21 above is followed, the second drilling will remove part of the intruding tenon and permit assembly if rails are inserted correctly. If stage 22 above is followed, the joint tenons will have to be partially mitred (see page 53).

FIG. 11

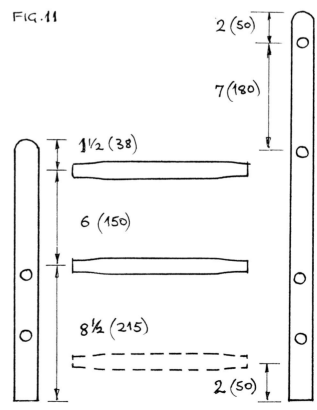

2 (50)

7 (180)

1½ (38)

6 (150)

8½ (215)

2 (50)

SECOND TRIAL ASSEMBLY

24 Check that individual side-rails fit sockets and go to full depth.

25 With back and front ladders assembled, add side-rails to complete main chair-frame.

26 Stand on level surface and check for stability. Adjust by careful twisting if required. When satisfied, mark parts for identification and disassemble.

MARKING AND DRILLING FOR BACK SPINDLES

27 Mark position of back spindle sockets on the two back cross-rails, ⅜in (9mm) in diameter, ½in (12mm) deep (Fig 12).

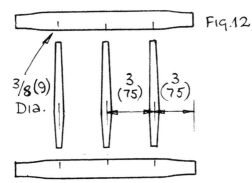

28 Drill sockets, keeping them in line.

29 Try spindles for fit and have trial assembly between the two back uprights.

First stage assembly; two 'ladders'

Second stage assembly; joining with side rails. (Note the protected bench top)

FINAL ASSEMBLY

30 Clean off all unwanted marks; smooth components (not seat-rails). Apply sanding sealer and sand smooth, or see alternative finish, below.

31 Assemble in correct sequence: begin by gluing three back spindles into cross-rails to make a 'sub-unit'.

32 Next assemble back ladder. Put glue into sockets, and insert previously glued sub-unit and other two rails, all to full depth. Check for wind.

33 Now assemble front ladder: put glue into sockets, insert rails to full depth, and check for wind.

34 Finally add side-rails: put glue into sockets, insert rails to full depth. Tap or press all together.

35 Stand on level surface and check for stability. Correct if necessary; wipe off surplus glue.

MAKING ROCKERS

36 Make rockers as in Fig 13. Saw to shape.

37 Round over front and back ends; lightly chamfer or round over sides to remove sharp edges.

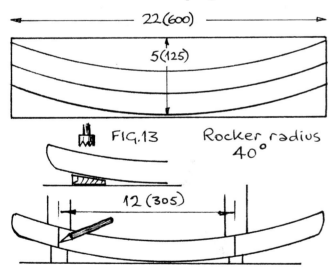

NOTE: The radius of 40in (1,020mm) required to mark out rockers may be drawn using a piece of cord tied to a pencil and held central to the arc. Keep the cord tight when marking out the curves. It is less wasteful of wood to cut rockers in pairs, as shown in Fig 13 and sizes given in cutting list allows for this.

FITTING ROCKERS

38 With chair standing on a level surface, place rockers alongside legs and mark position of joint sockets into rockers (see Fig 13). Distance between sockets should be 12in (305mm), but check this.

39 Drill sockets vertically at marked places, 1in (25mm) diameter, 1⅛in (28mm) deep. Block up rocker with a wedge when drilling to ensure drill enters correctly.

40 Trial-fit rockers; check for a smooth rocking movement, then remove. Apply sealer if required.

41 Put glue into sockets. Fit rockers to full depth. Clean off any surplus glue and leave to dry.

FINISHING

42 Final finishing and polishing is left until after the seat is woven.

43 When this is completed, with sealer previously applied, rub down gently and apply wax polish. If an alternative finish is preferred apply two or three coats of thinned polyurethane. Keep all finishing materials off the woven seat.

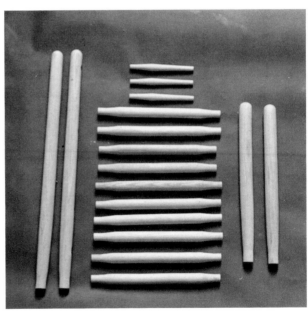

Child's rush-seat chair parts

No.	ITEM	INCHES	mm
	CHILD'S RUSH-SEAT CUTTING LIST (Add waste)		
2	Back uprights	25 × 1½ × 1½	635 × 38 × 38
2	Front uprights	16 × 1½ × 1½	410 × 38 × 38
10	Rails	12 × 1 × 1	305 × 25 × 25
3	Back spindles	7 × ¾ × ¾	108 × 19 × 19
1	For 2 rockers	22 × 5 × 1½	560 × 125 × 38

Comb-Back

Early 'Windsor' chairs were made to what is generally known as the 'comb back' design, the name coming from the resemblance of the top rail and back to a large comb, the earliest having mainly stick-backs without the central splat. In some examples the comb shows, in simplified form, the influence of the earlier, elaborate cresting rail of Restoration chairs, including the use of 'ears' to terminate the ends. In the style of chair where the comb is wider than the seat, the name 'fan-back' is sometimes applied.

When it was first introduced, the vertical rail up the centre of the back – known variously as the splat, baluster or banister – was unpierced, and simply shaped to a vase or urn profile. This, too, appears to have links with earlier, more elegant chair styles. In due course ornamentation in the form of piercing or fretting became popular, and the wheelback design most of all (see page 96).

Legs were sometimes spokeshaved, sometimes lathe-turned, and were fitted into the chair seat at a rakish angle for stability, the earliest without the benefit of stretchers. Where stretchers were fitted they were placed low down between the legs. Distinctive features of the turned legs and stretchers of this period were, first, the vase and ball design emphasised low on the front legs only (back legs usually being left plain), and the so-called arrowhead shape of the cross-stretchers.

Many of these features are incorporated into the chair described here; it is of the single or side variety, and the construction includes both through – and blind leg joints. These were sometimes used in combination during the early eighteenth century, which is perhaps indicative of the transition from the one form of jointing to the other during this period.

The completed chair was painted, as was fashionable for these chairs at the time because of their popular use as garden furniture. And with painting in view the chair was made with a variety of woods: elm for the seat, beech for the comb and legs, ash for everything else.

Eighteenth-century comb-back chair in the Bodleian Library, Oxford

Recipe

CUTTING AND SHAPING SEAT

1 Mark out and cut seat to pattern in Fig 14.

2 The seat is lightly hollowed and the front edge rounded over for comfort. Use any safe, suitable method; see page 34.

3 Smooth off edges all round, and lightly chamfer top and bottom edges.

MARKING OUT AND DRILLING SEAT FOR LEGS

4 Mark out underside of seat for front leg sockets. These do not go through the seat; they are blind holes. Draw in alignment lines as in Fig 14.

5 Drill these two holes, 1in (25mm) diameter, 1⅛in (28mm) deep at angle of 12°.

6 Mark out top of seat for back leg sockets; these go through the seat. Draw in alignment lines as in Fig 14.

7 Drill these two holes right through the seat, 1in (25mm) diameter, at angle of 24°. If using sloping/hinged platform method, reverse platform before drilling to obtain correct orientation.

MARKING AND DRILLING SEAT FOR TOP COMPONENTS

8 Mark socket positions for back uprights, back-sticks and centre splat on top surface of seat.

9 Drill back-stick sockets, ¾in (19mm) diameter, 1in (25mm) deep at angle of 10°. Other sockets, which are rectangular, are also made at 10° angle. See this page for details, and note below for method.

NOTE: When drilling leg sockets, drill must be used with care or set to depth-stop for front legs to prevent drill going through. For back legs remember that when drilling through-sockets the drilling angle is reversed. Back uprights are rectangular in shape and sockets are made to suit. They may be made by first drilling waste away, then chiselling to rectangular shape. Mortice for centre splat may be chain-drilled and finished by chiselling. Back upright sockets are made to suit uprights, and cut 1in (25mm) deep; centre splat mortice, ¾in (19mm) deep.

MAKING UPRIGHTS, STICKS AND CENTRE SPLAT FOR BACK

10 Cut uprights to size and taper as shown in Fig 15.

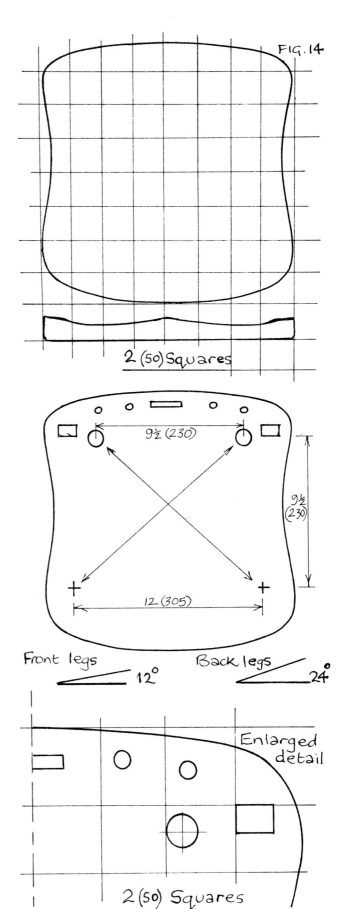

FIG. 14

2 (50) Squares

9½ (230)

9½ (230)

12 (305)

Front legs   12°   Back legs   24°

Enlarged detail

2 (50) Squares

Keep oversize initially, and fit lower ends individually into their respective sockets in seat. A slightly tapered fit gives this joint a neat appearance. Number, or otherwise identify them for ease of assembling later.

11 Turn or round the four back-sticks.

12 Cut centre back-splat to pattern.

13 Cut bottom joint carefully and try for a neat fit in mortice already cut in seat. Finally, round over edges and leave smooth.

MAKING, DRILLING AND FITTING COMB

14 Saw the vertical curve of the comb to pattern in Fig 15, but leave further shaping until after drilling.

15 Mark out underside of comb for back upright and back-stick sockets and centre splat mortice.

16 Drill the four back-stick sockets, ½in (12mm) diameter, ¾in (19mm) deep. Drill and chisel back upright sockets and centre splat mortice to required size, and all to ¾in (19mm) deep. All sockets and mortices are made vertically into the comb.

17 Complete shaping of comb to pattern; round over top edge and bring to a smooth finish.

18 Check that back uprights, back-sticks and centre splat are of required length, and try each individually for fit into sockets in comb.

19 Have a trial assembly of all top components: fit back uprights, back-sticks and centre splat into seat and add the comb. Everything should go together tight and under slight tension. When satisfied, disassemble for next stage.

MAKING LEGS AND STRETCHERS

20 Turn four legs and three stretchers to patterns and dimensions in Fig 16, or make by any other means. Keep stretchers generous in length at this stage. Check that joint diameters are correct and to full size.

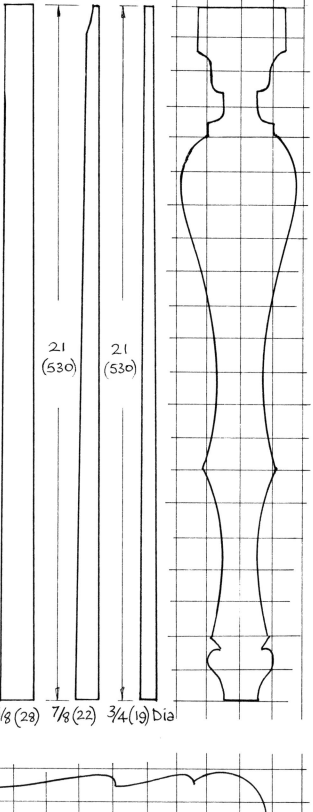

FIG.15

1 (25) 3/8 (9) ½ (12) Dia

21 (530) 21 (530)

1⅛ (28) 7/8 (22) ¾ (19) Dia

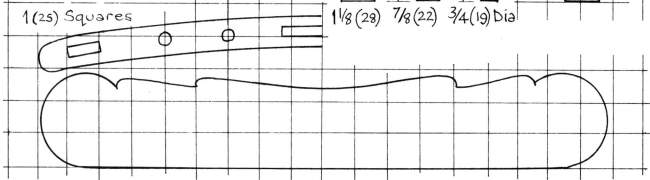

1 (25) Squares

21 Check legs for fit in respective sockets already drilled in seat.

FITTING LEGS AND STRETCHERS

22 With seat upside-down on protected bench, trial-fit legs into their respective sockets. Mark position of sockets for stretchers on each leg; remove legs and drill sockets ¾in (19mm) diameter, ¾in (19mm) deep. Angle for back legs is 17°, angle for front legs 6°. See note below, and method of drilling on page 100.

23 Insert legs back into correct seat sockets, push each side-stretcher to full depth in front leg socket, and with stretcher lying alongside the back leg, ascertain required length of each stretcher. Push legs apart whilst doing this to obtain maximum required length. Adjust length as necessary and replace stretchers.

24 Mark and drill socket in each side-stretcher for cross-stretcher, ¾in (19mm) diameter, ¾in (19mm) deep.

25 Refit side-stretchers into leg sockets, and repeat stage 23 to obtain length of cross-stretcher. Adjust to size.

26 Have trial assembly of legs and stretchers. See note below. Check on a level surface for rock or wobble. Adjust as necessary and disassemble.

NOTE: Stretchers are made overlength initially to allow proper fitting; they should stretch legs apart and all go together under slight tension. This can make assembly a little difficult, so use the following procedure. First insert legs part-way into their respective sockets; then with stretchers already assembled (as an 'H'), insert stretchers part-way into their sockets in legs, and push or tap with a soft mallet until everything is in place.

CLEANING UP AND FINAL ASSEMBLY

27 Make saw-cuts in top of back legs for wedges. Ensure wedges will be *across* grain of seat. Make the wedges.

FIG. 16   1 (25) Dia.   ¾ (19) Dia.

4½ (115) 17½ (445)

5 (125)

1¼ (32) Dia.

1¼ (32)

1¼ (32)

3 (75)

15½ (395)

2 off

18 (460)

18 (460)

Stretchers
1½ (38) Dia.   1 off

2 off   1¾ (44) Dia.   2 off

Fitting legs and stretchers (known as 'legging-up')

28 Clean up and smooth all components ready for assembly.

29 Begin by assembling underframe. With seat upside-down on protected bench, put glue into leg sockets in seat and into all stretcher sockets. Assemble as described in note above. Make sure all joints go fully home; back legs should protrude slightly through seat.

30 Stand upright on a firm surface, check for wobble and adjust if necessary. Insert wedges and hammer in tight. Wipe off any surplus glue.

31 Now assemble top components. Put glue into all sockets and mortices in seat; fit back uprights, back-sticks and centre splat into their respective places. Put glue into sockets and mortices in comb, and bring this down onto the other top components, manipulating each into its respective place. Check that all joints go fully home and that comb lies correctly. Wipe off any surplus glue and leave to dry and set.

FINISHING

32 This chair was given an antiqued paint finish. I used a paint made to an old recipe (see page 147 for suppliers) and began with an undercoat of dark red. When this was dry, a coat of dark green was applied and before this had quite dried it was rubbed through to the undercoat and to bare wood in some areas to imitate use and wear. Finally when this was fully dry, the chair was wax-polished to a dull gloss. This paint finish is not suitable for long exposure outdoors; for this, an oil-based paint should be used.

Test fitting back components and comb

Comb-back chair parts

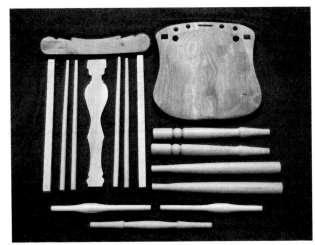

COMB-BACK		CUTTING LIST (Add waste)	
No.	ITEM	INCHES	mm
1	Seat	16 × 16 × 1¾	410 × 410 × 44
2	Front legs	17½ × 1¾ × 1¾	445 × 44 × 44
2	Back legs	18 × 1¾ × 1¾	460 × 44 × 44
2	Stretchers	15½ × 1½ × 1½	390 × 38 × 38
1	Stretcher	18 × 1½ × 1½	460 × 38 × 38
2	Back uprights	21 × 1⅛ × ⅞	530 × 28 × 22
4	Back-sticks	21 × ¾ × ¾	530 × 19 × 19
1	Back-slat	21 × 4 × ⅜	530 × 100 × 9
1	Comb	18 × 3 × 2	460 × 75 × 50

Single Ladderback

Ladderback is the general name given to any chair having flat, horizontal rails or slats between its back uprights. A fourteenth-century manuscript in the Bodleian Library in Oxford suggests that such chairs were known in medieval times; when rediscovered and reintroduced from Holland in the mid-seventeenth century they were known as Dutch chairs, whilst in America they became known as 'slatbacks'.

Over the years the design of the chair, and in particular the arrangement of the back, has taken many forms, from the simple rush-seated example described here, to more elaborate designs incorporating pad feet and panelled wooden seats with Cupid's bow and serpentine slats in any number from three to seven, some decreasing in width from top to bottom. The designers of the Chippendale period took them to extreme and used mahogany, while country makers continued to produce chairs in traditional styles in native timbers, until their 'rediscovery' yet again by the later protagonists of the Arts and Crafts Movement. During the nineteenth century they were most popular, especially in the Midlands and north of England where they were made literally in their thousands to supply a rapidly expanding population.

An important attribute of these chairs is their relative simplicity of construction. They consist largely of plain turned or rounded parts, except for the back-slats which are made from thin sections of wood bent to shape on a former after steam-heating. Back leg uprights may also be steamed and bent to improve the stability and comfort of the chair; but equally, they can be left unbent, which saves both time and effort. In English chairs the seat was almost always woven with rush, although one regional variation was to use willow, and another was to fit a thin panel of wood (see page 120). In America, wood splint or woven tape was used, the best examples being the work of the Shaker communities.

This chair was made entirely in ash, cleft whilst still green and partly shaped before seasoning, then completed and assembled when dry. Equally it may be made from straight-grained, seasoned sawn timber as described.

An eighteenth-century print showing simple ladderback chairs being rushed

72

RECIPE

MAKING BACK AND FRONT UPRIGHTS

1 Prepare the required material. Turn or shape by hand or use rotary planes.

2 Make two back uprights 1⅜in (35mm) diameter, 40in (1,020mm) long. Make two front uprights 1⅜in (35mm) diameter, 19in (480mm) long.

MAKING SEAT-RAILS

3 Traditionally the four seat-rails were cleft and whittled to shape; Fig 17 shows the required shape. This method ensures a strong, correctly shaped rail.

4 Alternatively seat-rails can be made as stretchers, described below.

MAKING STRETCHERS

5 Turn, or otherwise round the back stretcher, 17in (430mm) long, 1in (25mm) diameter, and the four side-stretchers, 18in (460mm) long, 1in (25mm) diameter. Side-stretchers are adjusted to correct length at stages 22–24.

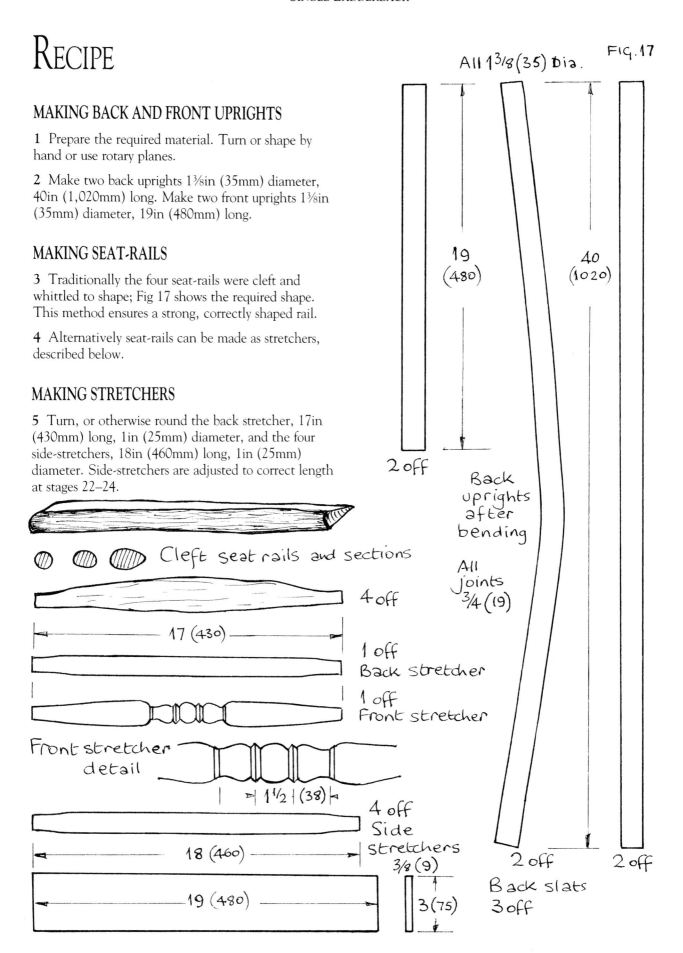

All 1⅜ (35) Dia.

FIG. 17

19 (480)

2 off

40 (1020)

Back uprights after bending

All joints ¾ (19)

2 off

2 off

Back slats 3 off

Cleft seat rails and sections

4 off

17 (430)

1 off Back stretcher

1 off Front stretcher

Front stretcher detail

1½ (38)

4 off Side stretchers ⅜ (9)

18 (460)

19 (480)

3 (75)

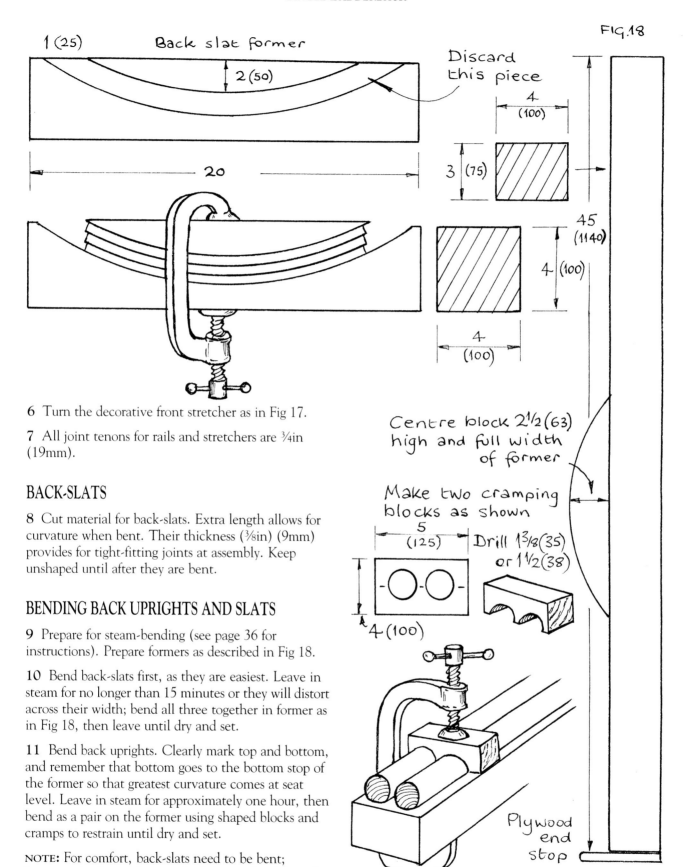

FIG.18

1 (25) Back slat former

2 (50)

20

Discard this piece

4 (100)

3 (75)

45 (1140)

4 (100)

4 (100)

Centre block 2½(63) high and full width of former

Make two cramping blocks as shown

5 (125)

Drill 1⅜(35) or 1½(38)

4 (100)

Plywood end stop

Back uprights former

6 Turn the decorative front stretcher as in Fig 17.

7 All joint tenons for rails and stretchers are ¾in (19mm).

BACK-SLATS

8 Cut material for back-slats. Extra length allows for curvature when bent. Their thickness (⅜in) (9mm) provides for tight-fitting joints at assembly. Keep unshaped until after they are bent.

BENDING BACK UPRIGHTS AND SLATS

9 Prepare for steam-bending (see page 36 for instructions). Prepare formers as described in Fig 18.

10 Bend back-slats first, as they are easiest. Leave in steam for no longer than 15 minutes or they will distort across their width; bend all three together in former as in Fig 18, then leave until dry and set.

11 Bend back uprights. Clearly mark top and bottom, and remember that bottom goes to the bottom stop of the former so that greatest curvature comes at seat level. Leave in steam for approximately one hour, then bend as a pair on the former using shaped blocks and cramps to restrain until dry and set.

NOTE: For comfort, back-slats need to be bent; however, back uprights may be left straight if desired. Bending them does improve both stability and comfort and is recommended; but if bending presents problems the chair can be made with the back uprights unbent.

MARKING OUT AND DRILLING UPRIGHTS (I)

12 Follow method of marking first a back 'ladder' and a front 'ladder', then joining these by means of side-rails as described earlier (page 62).

13 Back uprights, if bent, will lie naturally on a flat surface to give a left and a right component. Mark them as such. Front uprights (and straight back uprights) should be held in a 'V' cradle. Orientate for best grain figure in front, and mark as left and right.

14 Draw in a centre line on 'inside' surfaces of uprights and mark position of across-sockets only. Refer to Fig 19, left.

15 Using the 'V' cradle, drill these sockets ¾in (19mm) in diameter, ⅞in (22mm) deep and vertical.

16 Ensure sockets are 'in line' with each other by aligning drill with short length of dowel in first hole drilled, or use the sliding 'V' cradle and pillar drill for consistent alignment. See page 27.

FIRST TRIAL ASSEMBLY

17 Check that rails and stretchers are of correct length and that individual joints fit and go to full depth.

18 Then join the pairs of uprights to make a back ladder and a front ladder. Place on a flat surface and check for wind. Correct if necessary by gentle twisting.

MARKING OUT AND DRILLING UPRIGHTS (II)

19 With the two ladders still assembled and lying on a flat surface, mark position of side-rail and stretcher sockets. Refer to Fig 19. Note the staggered joints. Disassemble.

20 Using the 'V' cradle, drill these sockets ¾in (19mm) diameter, ⅞in (22mm) deep.

21 Keep sockets 'in line' as described above in stage 16, or use sliding 'V' cradle and pillar drill. Ensure that they are at 90° (right-angles) to previously drilled sockets. See note below. Support the arch of bent back uprights when applying drilling pressure to prevent risk of breakage.

NOTE: The staggered joints result in less weakening of the uprights, in particular the back ones at seat level. A 90° angle is ensured by placing a short length of tight-fitting ¾in (19mm) dowel into a previously drilled socket and placing a spirit level on it to check the angle. Use a similar aid if drilling by hand.

SIDE-RAILS AND STRETCHERS

22 Where back uprights are straight, the lengths of all side-rails and stretchers will be the same. With bent uprights they will differ in length, *ie* the further down they are, the longer they will have to be, because of the backward splay of the uprights.

23 Check these lengths by joining a front and a back upright with just one correct length side seat-rail, 17in (430mm) making sure joints go to full depth. Then with these parts lying on a flat surface, arrange as in Fig 19, right, and measure off required lengths of the remaining two stretchers.

24 Cut all four side-stretchers to required lengths, and mark for identification purposes.

SECOND TRIAL ASSEMBLY

25 Assemble back and front ladders as previously described, making sure all joints go to full depth.

26 Then add side-rails and stretchers to complete main chair-frame. Again, make sure all joints go to full depth.

27 Stand on level surface and check for stability. Adjust by gentle twisting if necessary.

MARKING OUT FOR BACK-SLATS

28 With chair-frame assembled, required length of back-slats can be ascertained. Check that the two back uprights are parallel to each other, then measure across back to mid-line of each back upright to obtain slat length measurement. Cut slats to length but be generous; trimming to exact length at fitting stage ensures good joints.

29 Disassemble chair frame and lay each back upright on a level surface, inner faces upwards. Mark position of each back-slat mortice on each upright. Refer to Fig 19, left.

NOTE: Back-slat mortices are marked to the *back* of the upright centre line (see Fig 19); this allows for the backward curvature of the slat at its point of entry into the back uprights, and is a very important constructional consideration.

CUTTING BACK-SLAT MORTICES

30 These may be cut by any available method, entirely by chiselling as in traditional hand-morticing, or chain-drilling followed by chiselling. A power router fitted with a suitable cutter used in combination with a

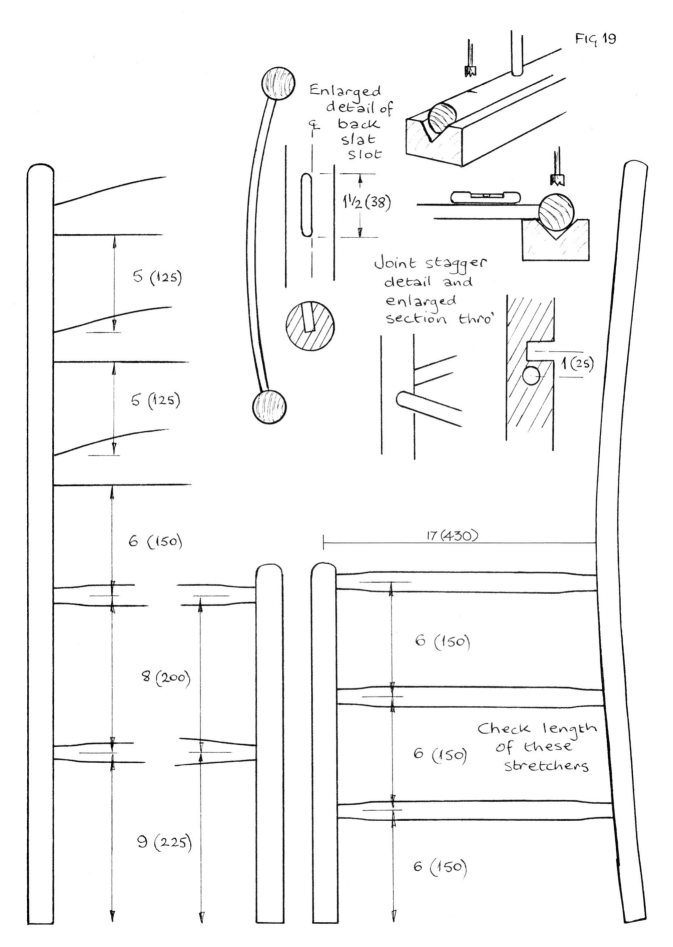

Fig 19

Enlarged detail of ℄ back slat slot

1½ (38)

Joint stagger detail and enlarged section thro'

1 (25)

5 (125)

5 (125)

6 (150)

17 (430)

6 (150)

8 (200)

6 (150)

Check length of these stretchers

9 (225)

6 (150)

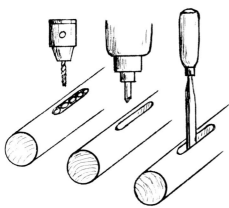

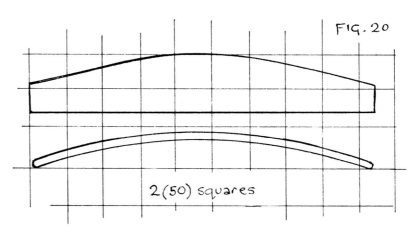

FIG. 20

2 (50) squares

Cut back-
slat mortices by any
available method

Fitting the back-slats

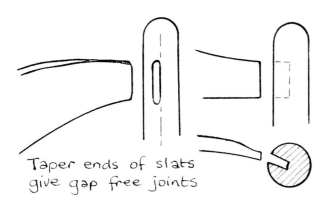

Taper ends of slats
give gap free joints

purpose-made jig is an alternative. The use of a chair-maker's or slot morticing bit is recommended. See pages 41 and 93 and above.

31 Cut mortices ¼in (6mm) wide, ¾in (19mm) deep, and for this chair 1½in (38mm) long. Keep ends of slots rounded to comply with the slats which are given rounded edges.

SHAPING AND FITTING BACK-SLATS

32 Shape slats to pattern, Fig 20. Retain slightly tapering ends which, together with some shaving of the back surface, provide for a gentle 'crush' fit and neat, gap-free joints (again, see Fig 20). Trim and fit each slat individually and number accordingly. This operation requires practice but produces very satisfying results when properly done.

33 When both ends of each slat have been individually fitted, assemble all components into back uprights to make a complete back ladder. Check for width across back, adjusting length of slats if necessary to obtain correct parallel measurement.

THIRD TRIAL ASSEMBLY

34 Assemble front ladder; add side rails and side stretchers to make complete chair frame.

35 Ensure all joints go to full depth. Stand on level surface and check for wobble and any tendency to twist. Adjust as necessary. When satisfied, disassemble.

NOTE: This final trial assembly or 'dry run' is recommended for all chairs, to ensure everything goes together correctly and to eliminate possible problems at the gluing-up stage.

CLEANING UP AND ASSEMBLING

36 Clean up all components, removing unwanted marks, but retain identification marks and numbers, otherwise assembly will cause problems. Tenons should be marked unobtrusively on their ends which will not be seen after gluing up.

37 A coat of sanding sealer may be applied, as described on page 41. There is no need to apply sealer to the seat-rails. Also, keep off joint areas.

The completed chair frame in the workshop

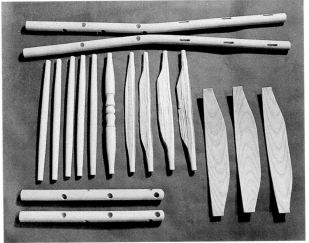

Single ladderback chair parts

40 Put glue in correct sockets and mortice slots in back uprights, then put in stretcher, seat-rail and slats. Push or press everything together to full depth. Lay on level surface and check for wind; twist gently to adjust if necessary. Remove surplus glue.

41 Now put glue in remaining sockets, and position correct side-stretchers and seat-rails to complete the chair-frame. Check that these last joints have all gone to their full depth, stand upright on a level surface and check for wobble. Remove surplus glue and leave to dry and set.

38 Assemble in sequence: first front ladder, then back ladder, then add side-rails and stretchers.

39 Put glue in correct sockets in front uprights, and add stretcher and seat-rail. Press all together to full depth, lay on level surface and check for wind. Remove surplus glue.

FINISHING

42 If components were sealed and sanded earlier, there is no need for further finishing until after the seat has been woven. After this, the chair-frame may be given a wax finish. If the chair is to be stained, this should be applied before the chair seat is woven (see page 42).

No.	ITEM	INCHES	mm
2	Back uprights	40 × 1⅜ × 1⅜	1020 × 35 × 35
2	Front legs	19 × 1⅜ × 1⅜	480 × 35 × 35
4	Seat-rails	17 × 1 × 1	430 × 25 × 25
1	Back stretcher	17 × 1 × 1	430 × 25 × 25
4	Side-stretchers	18 × 1 × 1	460 × 25 × 25
1	Front stretcher	17 × 1½ × 1½	430 × 38 × 38
3	Back-slats	19 × 3 × ⅜	480 × 75 × 9

SINGLE LADDERBACK CUTTING LIST (Add waste)

LOW BOW-BACK

The comb-back chair described earlier was frequently made as an armchair, this usually accomplished by the addition of a horizontal hoop or bow around the back of the chair parallel to the seat. The back-sticks passed through holes in the bow and on up to the comb, while additional side-sticks supported and held the bow in place. Not only did this provide armrests, but it substantially improved the construction by strengthening the back.

The hoop was made either by construction or by bending. The first is the earliest method and involves sawing out three separate pieces which, when joined together by means of overlapping joints (carpenter's half-laps), form the required curve without the problems associated with short grain, problems which prevent the hoop from being sawn in one piece. In due course hoops *were* made in one piece, by bending a straight-grained length of suitable wood after rendering it temporarily pliable by immersion in boiling water or steam.

On some chairs the horizontal hoop was used by itself, that is, without the comb rising above it, to make a low-back chair such as the one described here. A number of primitive, probably seventeenth-century Welsh and Irish chairs were of this form, the earliest extant examples usually having the three-piece arm construction, some quite crudely jointed. Further examples occur from Buckinghamshire and elsewhere dating from around the mid-nineteenth century, and again at the beginning of the present century when, as children's chairs, they were extensively used in schools. A 1920 catalogue claimed the chairs 'Are supplied in hundreds to the Council Schools and highly recommended by His Majesties Inspectors for hygiene purposes'. In those days they cost thirty shillings a dozen (£1.50 for twelve in today's terms).

The earlier examples are obvious prototypes for the later, more elaborate low-back Windsors such as the smoker's bow (see page 128), while the addition of a second bow above the horizontal hoop led to the development of the double bow Windsor style (see page 136). This chair therefore represents an intermediary design linking comb-backs to the later bow-back styles and provides a useful stepping stone between the two, both historically and constructionally.

In the chair described, both methods of producing the hoop or bow are outlined and either may be employed. Elm was used for the seat, ash for everything else. The size is suitable for children and small adults.

Early Welsh low-back chair

CHILD'S BOW-BACK & HEAD-BACK CHAIRS.

No. 20

As supplied in hundreds to the Council Schools, and highly recommended by H.M. Inspectors for Hygienic purposes.

30 - Doz.

Trade card (1920) showing a child's low-bow chair

RECIPE

MAKING BACK-BOW

1 This can be either a three-piece joined construction; or a single piece, steam-bent component.

2 For the joined construction see Fig 21, and from this make full-size patterns of the three shaped pieces. Use these as templates to mark out the required pieces on a 1½in (38mm) thick board with grain direction as shown.

3 Cut out these pieces; mark out and carefully cut the half-lap joints, checking for an accurate fit.

4 Accurate assembly is assisted by the use of a full-size pattern of the completed bow drawn on paper or thin card. Lay the three separate pieces on this to check jointing and shape. Pay particular attention to the angle of the lap joint ends: aim for a neat, gap-free fit.

5 When satisfied, glue parts together and hold with cramps until set. Do not worry about irregularities at this stage.

6 When set, clean up any irregularities, marrying the once separate pieces into a smooth continuous whole. Finish to profile shown.

7 For the single piece bow, first make the former for bending to the pattern in Fig 21.

8 Select and prepare the wood required for bending.

9 Bend the bow: refer to page 36 for instructions on steam-bending. Leave until properly dry and set.

NOTE: Retain the paper pattern for further use, see stage 22. The making of formers for bending purposes is described on page 26. The former made for this chair is similar to that described for the single bow Windsor, page 98, and could be re-used if that chair is made.

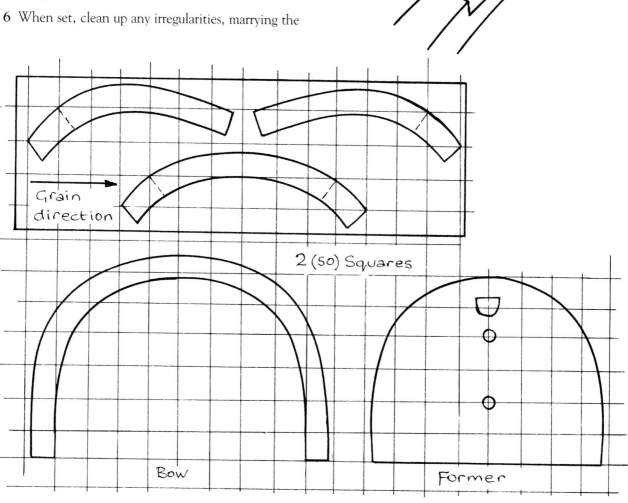

FIG. 21

Joint detail

Grain direction

2 (50) Squares

Bow

Former

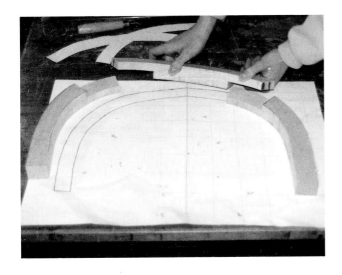

Parts of the back-bow on a full-size paper pattern

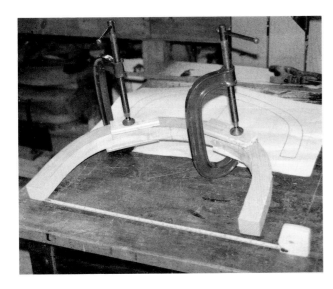

The joined back-bow in cramps after gluing

Steam bent back-bow on the bending former

SEAT SHAPING

10 Mark out seat shape to pattern given and cut by hand or with a bandsaw. If seat cannot be made from a single piece of wood, then narrower pieces may be edge-joined together by careful planing followed by gluing and cramping. See Fig 22.

11 Clean up and chamfer edges. Surface may be left flat or, preferably, hollowed for comfort – this need not be deeply, but front edges should be well rounded over. Use any method for hollowing; see page 34 for advice.

FIG.22

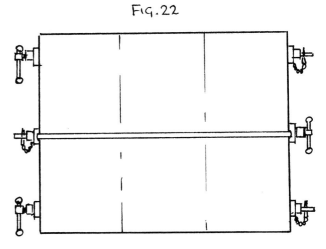

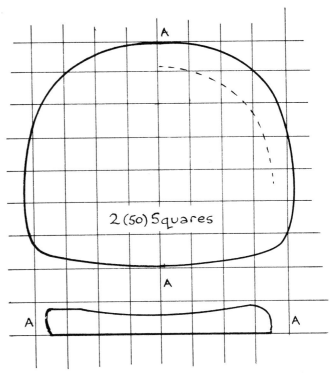

2 (50) Squares

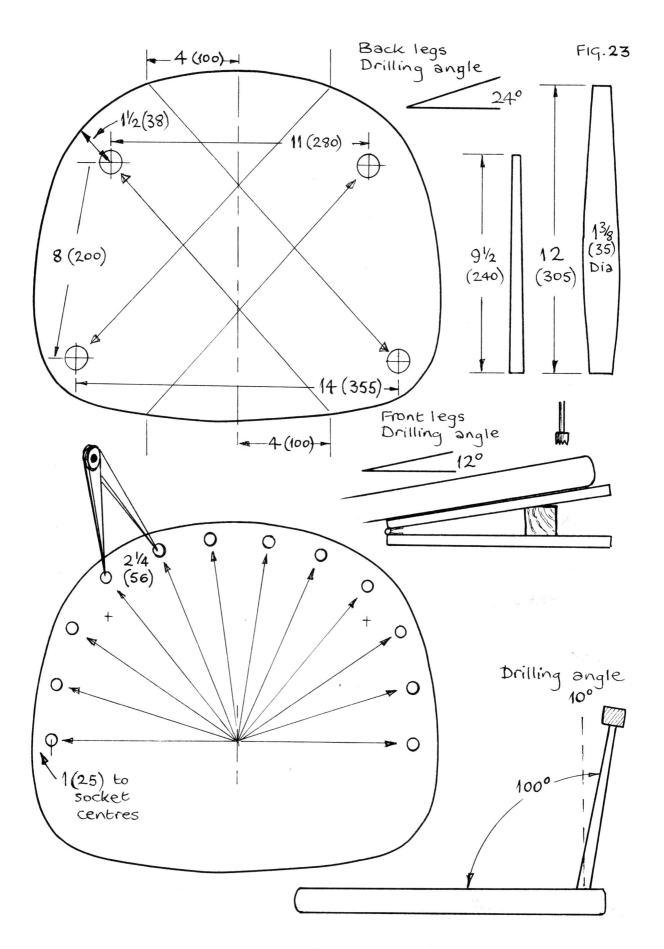

Fig. 23

Back legs
Drilling angle
24°

4 (100)

1½ (38)

11 (280)

8 (200)

14 (355)

4 (100)

9½ (240)

12 (305)

1⅜ (35) Dia

Front legs
Drilling angle
12°

2¼ (56)

1 (25) to socket centres

Drilling angle
10°

100°

MARKING OUT AND DRILLING FOR LEGS

12 On underside of seat, mark out position of leg sockets and draw in alignment or sight lines according to Fig 23.

13 Drill these four sockets, 1in (25mm) in diameter, 1⅛in (28mm) deep, back legs at angle of 24°, front legs at 12°. See page 38 for drilling methods.

MAKING AND FITTING LEGS

14 Turn the plain legs on a lathe, or use rounders, or shape with a spokeshave; any one of these methods is suitable, provided joint area is made a good fit in the 1in (25mm) diameter sockets in the seat. See Fig 23.

15 Check legs are of equal length, then with seat upside-down on a protected bench, try legs to their full depth, orientating them individually so that the best, rising grain figure faces forward.

16 Stand chair on a level surface and check that it does not rock or wobble. The seat surface will slope back slightly. Correct any faults before proceeding. When satisfied, mark legs for identification purposes, and disassemble.

NOTE: The backward slant of the seat, just a few degrees, is a desirable feature and is a natural outcome of the difference in angle between front and back legs, the greater angle at the back effectively shortening the vertical height. Because they are short, the legs do not require stretchers.

MARKING OUT AND DRILLING TOP OF SEAT

17 Mark out position of sockets for back-sticks, and draw in alignment or sight lines according to Fig 23.

18 Drill back-stick sockets, ¾in (19mm) diameter, 1in (25mm) deep, all at angle of 10°. See page 38 for drilling methods.

MAKING AND FITTING BACK-STICKS

19 Turn the plain back-sticks on a lathe, or use rounders or shape with a spokeshave. Taper from ¾in (19mm) to ½in (12mm) in diameter. See Fig 23.

20 Check back-sticks are of equal length and try for size in sockets drilled in seat.

Drilling the seat for the top components. (Note alignment lines)

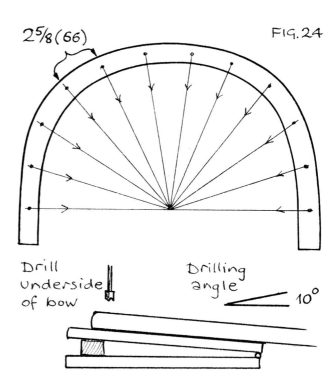

MARKING OUT AND DRILLING BACK-BOW

21 Mark position of back-stick sockets on underside of bow.

22 Alignment or sight lines are the same as those used when drilling the corresponding sockets into seat. Draw these on the full-size pattern used in stage 4 and extend on to bow surface as an aid to drilling.

23 Drill the sockets, ½in (12mm) diameter, ¾in (19mm) deep, all at angle of 10°.

FITTING BACK-BOW

24 When completed, and with back-sticks rising from seat, lower back-bow onto sticks, starting at the back and manipulating sticks into their respective sockets in bow. Press down or tap with a soft mallet until top surface of bow is 9in (230mm) above seat surface and parallel to it. Orientate individual back-sticks so that the best, rising grain shows. When satisfied, disassemble.

NOTE: The extra depth of back-stick sockets into seat not only ensures a sound joint, but also allows for any adjustment necessary to bring bow properly parallel to seat surface when assembling.

NOTE: The drilling angle for back-sticks is the same in both seat and bow, but because the bow sockets are into the underside of the bow, the angle is now opposite and the alignment is reversed. See Fig 24. The

Drilling the underside of the seat bow

Low bow-back chair parts

drilling and fitting procedure as described is common to other chairs and is a useful learning exercise.

PREPARATION FOR ASSEMBLY

25 Clean up and smooth all parts. Leave any identification marks (in an inconspicuous place) to help with component recognition at assembly.

26 As described in Finishing, page 41, there are advantages in part-finishing components before assembly. If this method is to be followed, apply sanding sealer. Keep off joint areas. Lightly sand when dry and prepare for assembly.

ASSEMBLY AND FINISHING

27 With seat upside-down on a protected surface, put glue into leg sockets and insert legs, correctly orientated, then push or tap down to full depth. Stand on level surface and check for wobble. Correct if necessary.

28 Put glue into back-sticks sockets in seat surface. Partly insert sticks, orientate correctly. Put glue into sockets in arm-bow and bring this down onto sticks as described.

29 Push or tap fully home, checking that bow is parallel to seat surface. Remove any surplus glue and leave to dry.

30 With all components previously sealed and sanded, a minimum of two applications of wax polish, well rubbed, will bring the completed chair to a fine finish. See page 42 for finishing information.

LOW BOW-BACK CUTTING LIST (Add waste)			
No.	ITEM	INCHES	mm
1	Seat	17 × 14 × 1½	430 × 355 × 38
4	Legs	12 × 1⅜ × 1⅜	305 × 35 × 35
12	Back-sticks	9½ × ¾ × ¾	240 × 19 × 19
1	(for bent bow)	36 × 1¼ × 1¼	920 × 32 × 32
	(or for joined bow see Fig 21)		

CLISSETT LADDERBACK

This chair is named after a nineteenth-century chairmaker, Philip Clissett: born in 1817, he started making chairs in about 1838, and was still making them when he was an old man at over ninety years of age. Clissett lived and worked near Bosbury in the county of Herefordshire, and was one of a family of chairmakers who worked in and around that area.

For most of his life he made mainly spindleback chairs with inset wooden seats in the traditional style of the region, and it was not until towards the end of the nineteenth century, when he was in his seventies, that he is thought to have made this rush-seated ladderback style which today bears his name. Significantly, he appears to have adopted the style during his involvement with certain designers associated with the Arts and Crafts Movement, and it is possible that they introduced Clissett to this 'new' design, one already common to other chairmakers in the region.

Whatever the case, the Clissett-'style' low back, rush-seated ladderback armchair, to give it its full descriptive title, is a worthy example of a traditional English country chair. Distinctive in being rather lower in the back than more familiar ladderbacks, its simple lines are enhanced by the graceful sweep of its arms. In particular its components reflect the means of production, its round parts, traditionally cleft and shaped on the pole lathe, being just plain turnings without decoration, the back-slats and arms the product of handwork with the drawknife. The chair's simplicity displays strong associations with American Shaker styles.

Ash is the correct wood to use, and if cleft material is available this would be ideal; but straight-grained, sawn ash is also suitable. The two back uprights and the three back-slats are steam-bent, and these should preferably be from air-dried and not kiln-dried material.

Directions for making the Clissett armchair are given, but a matching chair without arms can be made to the same recipe and dimensions simply by reducing the length of the two front uprights and omitting the arms.

Late nineteenth-century Clissett armchair

RECIPE

TURNED COMPONENTS

1 Turn or round the two back uprights, 1⅜in (35mm) in diameter, 38in (965mm) long. These will be bent. See stages 6 and 7.

2 Turn or round the two front uprights, 1⅜in (35mm) diameter, 28in (710mm) long, (or for the chair without arms, 19in (480mm) long).

3 Make two seat-rails, 1in (25mm) in diameter, 18½in (470mm) long.
Make two seat-rails, 1in (25mm) in diameter, 16½in (420mm) long.
Make four front and back stretchers ¾in (19mm) in diameter, 18½in (470mm) long.
Make four side stretchers ¾in (19mm) in diameter, 18½in (470mm) long. These last stretchers are purposely overlength and will be adjusted at stages 19 to 22.

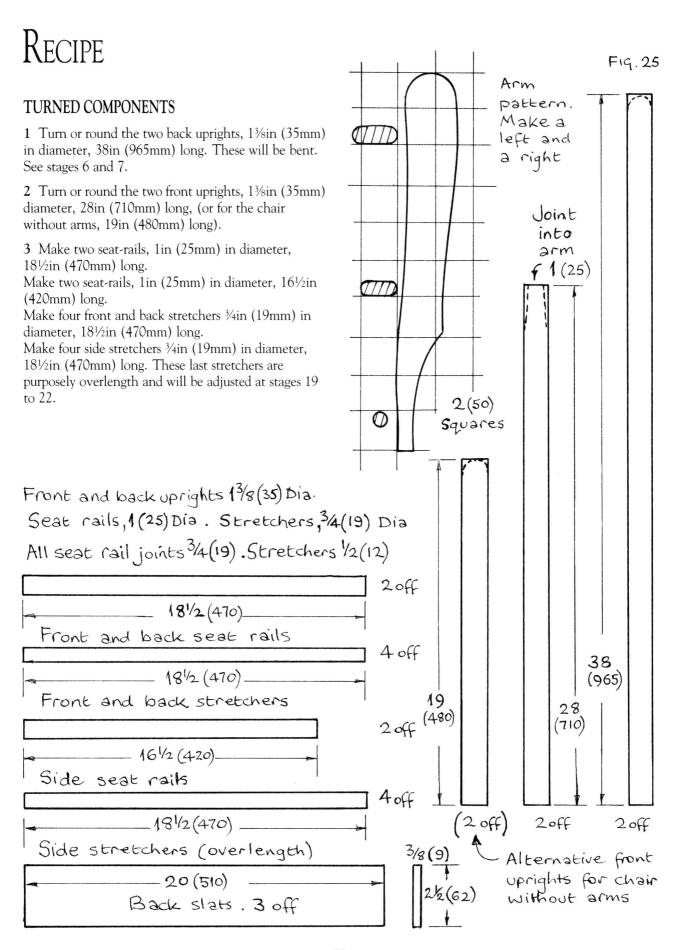

Fig. 25

Arm pattern. Make a left and a right

Joint into arm

ʄ 1 (25)

2 (50) Squares

Front and back uprights 1⅜ (35) Dia.

Seat rails, 1 (25) Dia . Stretchers, ¾ (19) Dia

All seat rail joints ¾ (19). Stretchers ½ (12)

2 off

18½ (470)

Front and back seat rails

4 off

18½ (470)

Front and back stretchers

2 off

16½ (420)

Side seat rails

4 off

18½ (470)

Side stretchers (overlength)

20 (510)

Back slats . 3 off

19 (480)

28 (710)

38 (965)

(2 off)   2 off   2 off

3/8 (9)

2½ (62)

Alternative front uprights for chair without arms

90

BACK-SLATS

4 Cut material for back-slats, see Fig 25. These, too, are overlength to allow for curvature after bending. For now, keep them rectangular and of equal width to simplify the bending.

ARMS

5 Cut a pair of arms to pattern in Fig 25; simply turn pattern over to make left and right arms. Try to balance grain marking in each arm by 'bookmatching'. (See Glossary.)

BENDING BACK UPRIGHTS AND BACK-SLATS

6 Prepare for steam-bending. The necessary formers are the same as those used for the single ladderback chair described on page 75, Fig 18.

7 Follow instructions given for steam-bending on page 36.

SHAPING ARMS

8 First taper back ends, and round to a ¾in (19mm) joint for fitting into back uprights. This can be done by careful spokeshaving or by using appropriate-sized rounders (see page 32).

9 Then shape and smooth each arm until they have a matching 'comfortable' feel and appearance. Emphasise rounding over on top inside edge, and leave full and flat underneath at front for jointing purposes.

NOTE: The concept of shaping the arms until they have a comfortable feel and appearance is an obvious one, but not easy in the beginning to achieve in practice. Look at and feel the arms on other chairs to get an idea of what you find satisfactory, and use this as a guide. The profiles given in Fig 25 should help.

MARKING OUT AND DRILLING UPRIGHTS (I)

10 When back uprights are dry, remove from former and, together with front uprights, mark out for those rail and stretcher sockets which go across back and front of chair. Refer to Fig 26 for socket positions.

11 Mark uprights on centre line on their inside surfaces only. Back uprights, placed left and right on a flat surface, will lie naturally in position; front uprights should be held in a 'V' cradle. Orientate for best grain figure to front.

12 The object, as described previously on page 62, is to make first a back and a front 'ladder', then to join

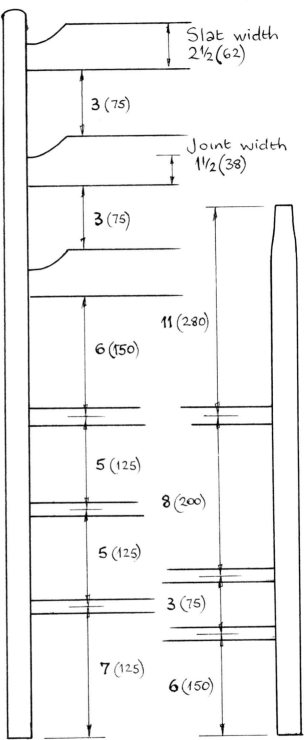

FIG. 26

Slat width 2½ (62)

3 (75)

Joint width 1½ (38)

3 (75)

11 (280)

6 (150)

5 (125)

8 (200)

5 (125)

3 (75)

7 (125)

6 (150)

these by side-rails and stretchers to reduce possibility of error.

13 Drill the marked sockets, ¾in (19mm) in diameter, ⅞in (22mm) deep for seat-rails; ½in (12mm) in diameter, ⅞in (22mm) deep for stretchers. For constant alignment use a sliding 'V' cradle, or the short dowel method described on page 27.

FIRST TRIAL FIT

14 Check that rails and stretchers are of correct length, and try for fit individually; then assemble into appropriate sockets to make the two separate sections, a front 'ladder' and a back 'ladder'.

15 Place on a level surface and check for wind; adjust by gentle twisting if necessary.

MARKING OUT AND DRILLING UPRIGHTS (II)

16 Whilst the two sections are assembled mark out position of side seat-rail and stretcher sockets on centre line. Refer to Fig 27.

17 Drill the marked sockets, ¾in (19mm) diameter, ⅞in (22mm) deep for seat-rails, ½in (12mm) diameter, ⅞in (22mm) deep for stretchers. Ensure that these sockets are drilled at 90° to previously drilled sockets. See note below. Support arch of back upright when drilling.

18 Sockets for arms should be drilled at this stage. Drill with top portion of back upright held horizontal to give slight upward angle when chair is assembled. Drill arm sockets ¾in (19mm) in diameter, ⅞in (22mm) deep.

NOTE: When drilling sockets, use the 'V' cradle and pillar drill if possible. To ensure 90° angle, place a short length of tight-fitting ¾in (19mm) dowel into a previously drilled seat-rail socket and place a spirit level or angle-finder (page 27) on it to check drilling angle. Use this method as a guide if drilling by hand.

SIDE-STRETCHERS AND TRIAL FIT

19 Because of the backward curve or backward splay of the leg portion of the back uprights, side-stretchers vary in length. Initially made overlength, they should now be adjusted.

20 Do this by temporarily joining a front and a back upright with a correct length seat-rail (16½in (420mm)), making sure joints go to full depth. Lie these on a flat surface and arrange as in Fig 27, and measure off required lengths. Cut stretchers to length.

21 Assemble front and back ladders as before; join together with side-rails and stretchers. Make sure all joints go to full depth.

22 Stand on a level surface and check for stability. Adjust by gentle twisting if necessary.

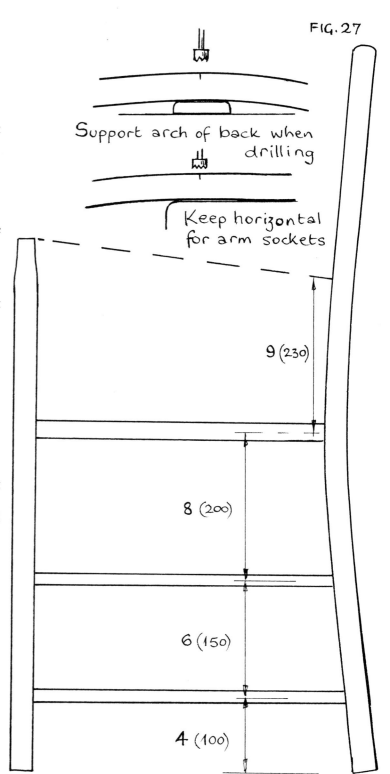

FIG. 27

Support arch of back when drilling

Keep horizontal for arm sockets

9 (230)

8 (200)

6 (150)

4 (100)

BACK-SLATS: MARKING OUT

23 With chair-frame assembled, correct length of back-slats can be ascertained. Measure across back to mid-line of each back upright.

24 Cut slats to length; be generous, and trim to size at fitting stage.

NOTE: Because of the curvature of the back-slats, the slot mortices into which they fit lie to the *back* of the upright centre line. This is very important; see Fig 28.

BACK-SLATS: MAKING SLAT MORTICES

25 Disassemble chair-frame and lie back uprights on level surface to mark out mortice positions. Refer to Fig 26.

26 Cut these mortices by any suitable means: for example, chain drilling followed by careful chiselling, or a router and suitable cutter. A chairmaker's or slot morticing bit is recommended (see page 39). Mortices are ¼in (6mm) wide, 1½in (38mm) long, ¾in (19mm) deep.

27 For accuracy and alignment use a sliding 'V' cradle (page 27). Keep ends of mortices rounded to suit rounded edges of slats.

BACK-SLATS: SHAPING AND FITTING

28 Shape slats to pattern in Fig 28. Round their edges and retain the slightly tapering ends which, together with some chamfering at the back, gives a gently 'crush' fit, and neat, gap-free joints. Trim and fit each slat individually, and mark or number accordingly.

29 When each slat fits individually, assemble complete back section, stretchers, seat-rail and slats, and on a level surface check for wind. Adjust if necessary.

ARMS: MEASURE AND FIT

30 Complete assembly of chair-frame by assembling front section and adding side components. Check that all joints go to full depth, stand on level surface and check for stability.

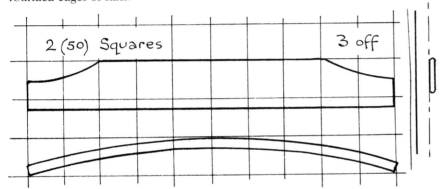
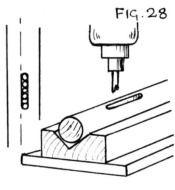

2 (50) Squares   3 off

FIG. 28

Cutting mortice slots for the back-slats

Shaping the arms, using a spokeshave

Fitting the arms

32 Remove arms and drill at marked places, 1in (25mm) diameter, 1in (25mm) deep. Do this carefully, but first see note below.

33 Try arms for fit. They should be pressed into place under tension. Ensure joints go to full depth. Check chair on a level surface again and when satisfied, disassemble.

NOTE: Because the arms angle slightly upwards they must be drilled at an angle; Fig 29 shows how this may be done. Note end tenon is highest when drilling.

CLEANING UP AND ASSEMBLING

34 Clean up all components, removing unwanted marks, but retain all identification marks.

35 Apply a coat of sanding sealer at this stage if required. Keep off joint areas. See page 41.

36 Assemble in sequence: first back section, then front section, then join together with side components.

37 Put glue in correct sockets and in the mortice slots in back uprights. Fit stretchers, seat-rail and back-slats and push fully home. Check on a level surface for wind.

38 Put glue in correct sockets in front uprights. Fit stretchers and seat-rail, push fully home and check as above.

39 Then put glue into remaining sockets (except arm sockets) and add correct stretchers and seat-rails.

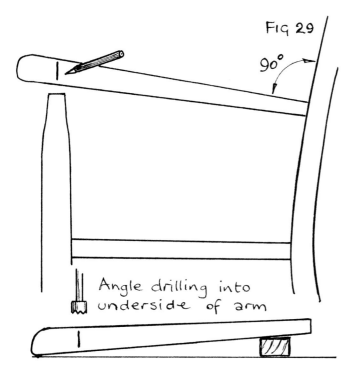

FIG 29

90°

Angle drilling into underside of arm

31 With chair-frame assembled, trial-fit arms fully into previously drilled sockets in back uprights. Allow to lie on top or to one side of uprising front uprights, and mark position for joint socket into underside of each arm. Offset slightly to front to ensure a tension fit, keeping back tenon well into back upright socket.

Ensure that these joints go fully home. Stand on a level surface and check stability. If joints are correctly made cramps will not be required, except perhaps to pull a tight joint together.

40 Finally, fit arms by first putting glue into sockets, enter end tenons fully into sockets in back uprights, and bring arms down onto front uprights. Press or tap down to a good fit.

41 Check again for stability. Clean off any surplus glue and leave to dry.

FINISHING

42 If components were sealed and sanded before assembly, nothing more need be done until after the seat is woven. After this the chair may be given a wax finish. Avoid getting wax on the woven seat material.

NOTES FOR CHAIR WITHOUT ARMS

43 To make a matching chair, or chairs, without arms, only slight modification is required.

44 The two front uprights should be made to the 19in (480mm) dimension given in Fig 25 and the tops rounded over.

45 Omit drilling the arm sockets in back uprights (stage 18).

46 And, of course, do not make the arms. All else is as described for making the companion armchair.

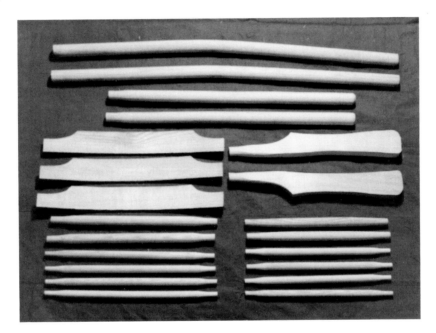

Clissett armchair parts

CLISSET LADDERBACK CUTTING LIST (Add waste)			
No.	ITEM	INCHES	mm
2	Back uprights	38 × 1⅜ × 1⅜	965 × 35 × 35
2	Front uprights	28 × 1⅜ × 1⅜	710 × 35 × 35
(2	Front legs	19 × 1⅜ × 1⅜	480 × 35 × 35)
2	Seat-rails	18½ × 1 × 1	470 × 25 × 25
2	Seat-rails	16½ × 1 × 1	420 × 25 × 25
4	Stretchers	18½ × ¾ × ¾	470 × 19 × 19
4	Stretchers	18½ × ¾ × ¾	470 × 19 × 19
3	Back-slats	20 × 2½ × ⅜	510 × 62 × 9
2	Arms	20 × 2½ × 1½	510 × 62 × 38

SINGLE BOW WINDSOR

This Windsor chair style is described variously as a single or side chair to differentiate it from the Windsor armchair, and was common throughout the entire nineteenth century. In Louden's *Encyclopedia of Cottage, Farm and Villa Architecture and Furniture* of 1833 the chair is described as 'one of the best kitchen chairs in use in the Midland counties of England. The seat is of elm, somewhat hollowed out; the outer rail of the back is of ash, in one piece, bent to the sort of horseshoe form shown in the figure, by being previously heated or steamed'.

The earliest examples seem to have been of the stick-back variety, as shown here, but it was not long before the ornamental centre splat, already popular in comb-back chairs, was introduced. This led in turn to the use of a particular splat motif, the wheel, which gave the well known name 'wheelback' to this type of chair.

The origin of this motif is obscure, but probably relates to the tradition that some early Windsor chairmakers were also wheelwrights. There are rare examples of chairs which have, within their back-bow, spindles radiating from a central hub as in a cartwheel, and many more which incorporate a central roundel in their splat design, considered to be the vestigial hub of a wooden wheel. The pierced wheelback splat is likely to be of this lineage.

As kitchen and dining-room chairs, both the stick-back and the wheelback have been in use for over two hundred years and are still popular today. They have been reproduced and redesigned innumerable times, and there are several versions, all of which may be bought in High Street shops everywhere; they are made in a variety of woods, some more unsuitable than others, and many are evidently manufactured worldwide.

It is the stick-back style which is featured here, and there is a full description on how to make this version of the chair properly. Additional instructions are given as to how it can also be made as a wheelback variant, both chairs having the same design for the seat and underframe, and the same size and shape of back bow. The chair shown was made in ash with an elm seat; beech could be an alternative.

Nineteenth-century single bow-back chair

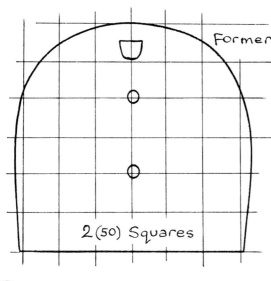

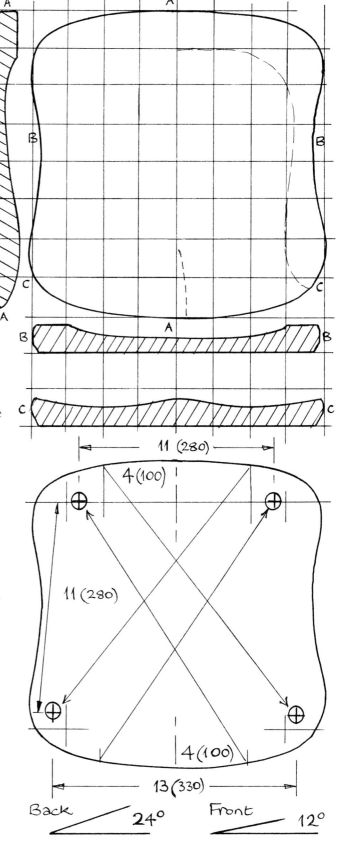

FIG. 30

Former

2 (50) Squares

RECIPE

BENDING BACK-BOW

1 Select and prepare the wood required.

2 Make and use the former shown in Fig 30. The former made for the low bow-back chair, would also be suitable. (See note, page 82.)

3 Bend the bow and leave to dry and set. Refer to page 36 for instructions on steam-bending.

CUTTING AND SHAPING SEAT

4 Cut seat to shape shown using hand-saw or bandsaw.

5 Mark out area to be hollowed, and rough this out using any suitable, safe method. See page 34 for details. Refer to the diagram for guide to seat profile (Fig 30). Keep full at front corners where leg sockets occur. Leave final finish until later.

6 Clean up and chamfer edges of seat.

MARKING OUT AND DRILLING LEG SOCKETS

7 Mark out position of leg sockets on underside of seat. Draw in alignment or sight lines. See Fig 30.

8 Drill the four sockets, 1in (25mm) in diameter, 1⅛in (28mm) deep, the back legs at angle of 24°, the front legs at 12° (Fig 32). See page 39 for recommended drilling method, or use any other method.

TURNED COMPONENTS

9 Lathe-turn the four legs and stretchers; keep joint areas accurately to size (see Fig 31). Make back-sticks by turning or 'rounding'. See page 32 for description of methods.

FITTING LEGS AND STRETCHERS

10 With seat upside-down on bench, check that legs fit tightly and fully into sockets in seat. Orientate so that best grain figure faces forward, and mark side-stretcher socket positions on inside surface of each leg. Mark legs for identification purposes. Remove legs.

FIG. 31

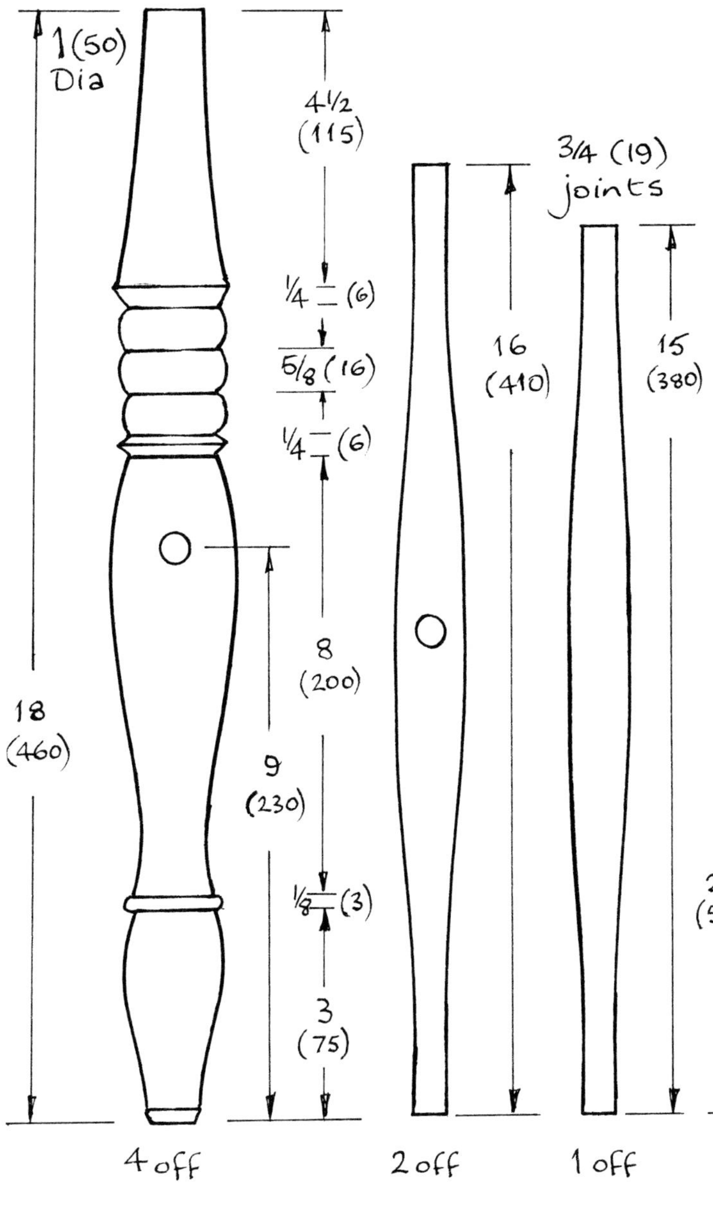

1 (50) Dia

4½ (115)

¼ (6)

5/8 (16)

¼ (6)

18 (460)

8 (200)

9 (230)

⅛ (3)

3 (75)

4 off

½ (12) Dia joints

¾ (19) joints

16 (410)

15 (380)

2 off

1 off

21 (535)

23 (585)

2 off (2)

3 off (2)

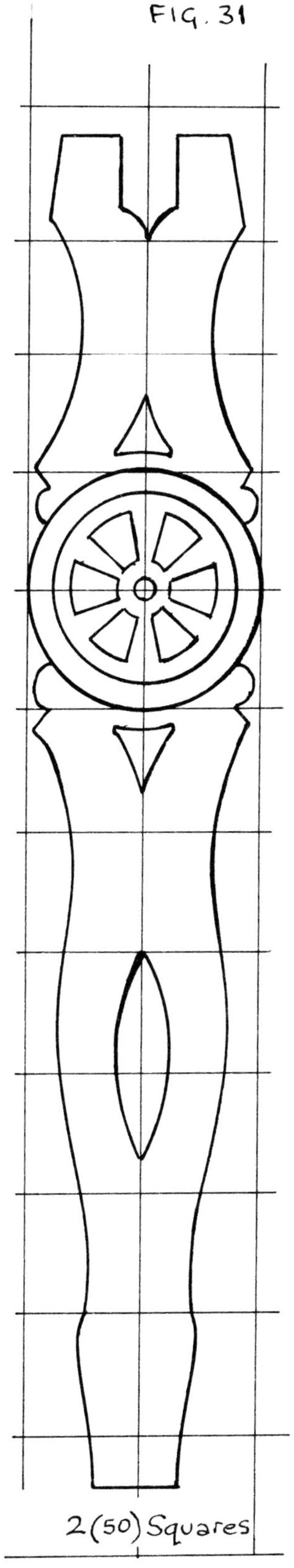

2 (50) Squares

Wheelback splat for alternative style of chair

99

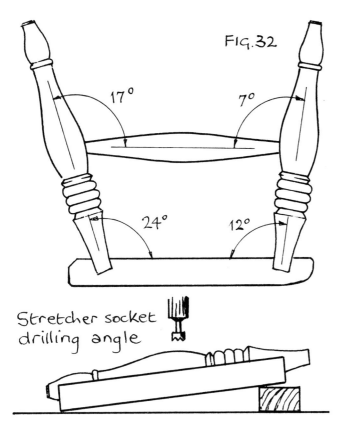

FIG. 32

17° 7°

24° 12°

Stretcher socket
drilling angle

11 Drill stretcher sockets into legs, ¾in (19mm) in diameter, ¾in (19mm) deep, back legs at angle of 17°, front legs at angle of 7° (Fig 32).

12 Refit legs into appropriate sockets (front and back legs are not now interchangeable) and add side-stretchers. See note below on assembly. Ascertain position and length of cross stretcher and mark its socket positions on side-stretchers. Remove these and drill, ¾in (19mm) in diameter, ¾in (19mm) deep.

13 Reassemble stretchers into legs, check that all joints go to full depth. Stand on level surface and check for wobble, and adjust if necessary. Identify all components and disassemble for next stage when satisfied.

NOTE: It may be necessary to adjust length of stretchers during trial assembly; they are purposely oversize initially. Remember, stretchers should stretch legs apart and should therefore *not* be cut too short. All should go together under slight tension. Assemble by first fitting legs but pushing only part-way into their sockets; then, with cross-stretcher already in place, add the stretchers and push or tap everything fully home.

MARKING AND DRILLING TOP OF SEAT

14 Mark out position of sockets for back bow and back-sticks. Draw in alignment or sight lines. See

Fig 33. (If wheelback is to be made, refer to same Fig for alternative marking out and drilling procedure.)

15 Drill back-bow sockets, ¾in (19mm) in diameter, right through seat at angle of 15°. Check angle and alignment carefully.

16 Drill back-stick sockets, ½in (12mm) in diameter, 1in (25mm) deep, at angle of 10°.

SHAPING AND FITTING BACK-BOW

17 Ascertain that back-bow is dry and set to shape. Cut to finished length if oversize, 58in (1,470mm), and reduce both ends to ¾in (19mm) diameter for approximately 3in (75mm).

18 Check for fit into sockets in seat, first individually, then jointly: the joints should not be too tight; the bow is sprung in under slight tension and should protrude a little below seat.

19 Remove bow, and shape to quadrant profile shown (Fig 34), neatly marrying this shape into the round ends.

FIG. 33

2¼ (58)   Wheelback
alternative

13 (330)

Back
stick
drilling
angle 10°

Sight
line for
back bow
~drill at 15°

7
(180)

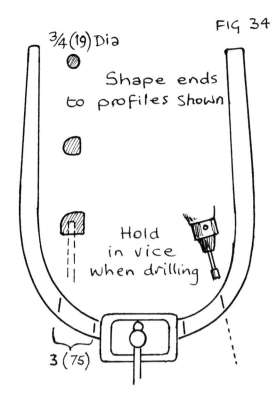

FIG 34

¾ (19) Dia

Shape ends to profiles shown

Hold in vice when drilling

3 (75)

ALIGNING BACK-STICKS

20 With back bow again in place, insert back-sticks a little over half-way into their sockets in seat and allow to lie to back of bow. Orientate for best grain figure to front.

21 Mark top centre of bow, align middle back-stick to this and arrange other sticks equally to each side. Mark socket positions on underside of bow; mark 'lie' of each stick on front surface of bow as an aid to drilling. See Fig 34.

22 Ascertain required length of each back-stick, identify and remove. Cut back-sticks to length; check that top joint area remains at ½in (12mm).

Measuring back-sticks for length

DRILLING BACK-BOW, AND FINAL TRIAL FIT

23 Remove bow and drill back-stick sockets. This stage relies partly on eye judgement, but see page 39 for advice on top bow drilling. Work carefully and do not go too deep. Check back-sticks individually for fit.

24 Replace back-sticks to previous depth; then add back-bow, inserting ends into seat and whilst pushing down, manipulate back-sticks into their respective sockets. Check that all goes together correctly, especially that ends of bow protrude slightly below seat. Tap down with a soft mallet if necessary.

NOTE: The extra depth of back-stick sockets in seat allows for some adjustment of back when assembling. Back-sticks are purposely overlength initially to facilitate marking out of their back-bow sockets; cutting to required length should be done carefully. All should fit tight and spring together under slight tension.

Drilling the back bow

FINAL PREPARATION

25 Make saw-cut 1in (25mm) deep in each end of back bow to accommodate wedges. Cut should lie *across* grain of seat. Make wedges. See Fig 35, and page 46.

26 Complete hollowing of seat and bring to a smooth finish. Clean up all other components; avoid tight-fitting joint areas.

27 All components may be sealed and sanded at this stage if required. See Finishing, page 41.

FINAL ASSEMBLY

28 With seat upside-down on protected surface, put glue into leg sockets in seat and into all stretcher sockets. Fit legs part-way into sockets, add stretchers, and push or tap everything down into place. Check all joints are fully home; stand on a level surface and check for stability. Wipe off any surplus glue.

29 Assemble back-bow and back-sticks. Put glue into all sockets in seat surface and insert back-sticks part-way. Put glue into sockets in back bow, insert bow into seat sockets and whilst pushing down manipulate back-sticks into place. Check all goes together correctly and adjust as necessary.

30 Invert seat on protected bench, fit wedges in protruding ends of bow and hammer in tight. See Fig 35. Do this before glue in joint sets. (Later, cut off stubs flush with seat bottom.) Wipe off any surplus glue, stand chair upright and leave until glue has set.

FIG. 35

Back bow wedging

FINISHING

31 Finish the chair as required, either natural or stained. See Finishing, page 42.

OPTION: WHEELBACK VERSION

32 Follow stages 1 to 13 (only four back-sticks are required); then mark out top of seat according to Fig 33. Drilling angles and alignments remain the same. The mortice slot for the back-splat is 1½in (38mm) long, ¼in (6mm) wide and ¾in (19mm) deep.

33 Cut out and clean up back-splat to pattern shown in Fig 31, page 99. Length measurement is generous and will require adjustment later. Trim and fit bottom joint.

34 Now refer to stages 17 to 22; fit back bow, and mark position of slot mortice for back-splat. Align back-sticks to wheelback positions and mark their 'lie' lines. Ascertain correct length of sticks and splat.

35 Remove bow, drill back-stick sockets and cut slot mortice. After cutting back-splat to length, trim top joint to fit.

36 Reassemble back-bow, back-sticks and back-splat as previously described, and continue through to stage 31.

Single bow-back chair parts

Setting-up for a wheelback version

SINGLE BOW WINDSOR CUTTING LIST (Add waste)			
No.	ITEM	INCHES	mm
1	Seat	16 × 16 × 1¾	410 × 410 × 44
4	Legs	18 × 2 × 2	460 × 50 × 50
2	Stretchers	16 × 1½ × 1½	410 × 38 × 38
1	Stretcher	15 × 1½ × 1½	380 × 38 × 38
1	(for back bow)	60 × 1⅛ × 1⅛	1525 × 28 × 28
5	Back-sticks	23 × ¾ × ¾	580 × 19 × 19
(4	Back-sticks	23 × ¾ × ¾	580 × 19 × 19)
(1	Back-slat	23 × 4 × ⅜	580 × 100 × 9)

ROCKING CHAIR

The origin of the rocking chair is obscure, but the style is thought to have developed concurrently in America and England towards the end of the eighteenth century. During the next century these chairs became extremely popular in many of the American states where, apparently, they were known as digestive chairs. They were less popular, however, in Victorian England where they were considered socially unacceptable and only approved of on 'medical grounds', presumably as an aid to the digestion.

Their early acceptance in America led to the development of specially designed rocking chairs such as the Boston Rocker, while in addition the Shaker communities made many of their ladderback chair types to rock. The Thonet range of bentwood chairs made in Austria in the mid-nineteenth century included rocking chairs in which the rockers were an integral part of the chair. In England there appear to have been few, if any, chairs especially designed for rocking; instead, chairs of an existing type simply had rockers fitted to them. Trade catalogues of the period reveal that it was common for chairmakers to hold stocks of the curved rails which constituted 'the rockers' and which, at the customers's request, could be fitted to any of their range of otherwise static chairs, both Windsor and ladderback types.

An examination of the stretcher arrangement of many nineteenth-century rocking chairs confirms that this practice was widespread even though it was, constructionally, not entirely satisfactory. The chair shown below left, illustrates this point: originally made as a static chair, it has the common and quite adequate 'H'-stretcher; with rockers added, however, this results in the side-stretchers becoming duplicated and unnecessary while the central cross-stretcher becomes inadequate. In fact as a rocking chair it would be much stronger with cross-stretchers between the two front legs and between the two back legs instead.

The chair described here was specially designed and made as a rocking chair and incorporates this more desirable stretcher arrangement. The chair is, by definition, a comb-back Windsor rocking chair, and although contemporary in concept, it embraces many traditional features and methods of construction. Made in ash with seat and comb in elm, it was finished by wax polishing. Notes are included on how it can be made as a static chair if required.

Spindle back rocking chair c1860

Trade card (c1880) offering rockers for 1 shilling (5p) extra

Recipe

TURNING LEGS, ARM-STUMPS, ETC

1 Turn four legs and two arm-stumps as in Fig 36. Individualise, but retain overall length and joint dimensions.

2 Turn or round the two stretchers as shown. Reduce lengths later as required.

3 Turn or round the five long back-sticks and the four shorter side-sticks. These are generous in length and will require some final adjustment.

MAKING AND JOINTING BACK UPRIGHT

4 Cut out two back uprights to pattern, Fig 37.

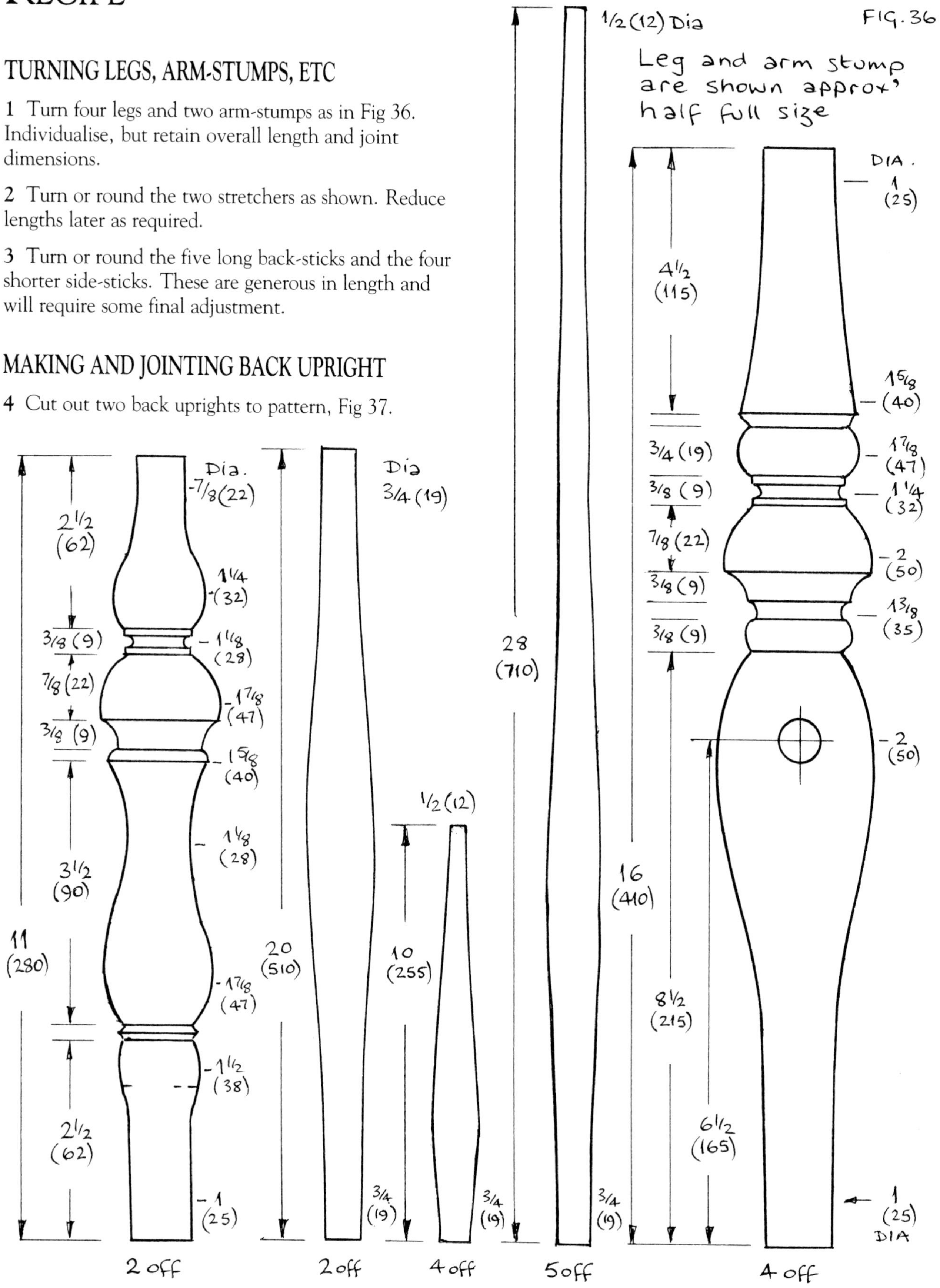

Fig. 36

Leg and arm stump are shown approx' half full size

5 The top finials and joints may be turned on the lathe by means of an appropriate technique. For this do not initially cut away the shaded portion of the pattern; this allows in-line centres to be marked as shown and the workpiece mounted in the lathe, finial end to headstock. Turn to pattern and remove excess (shaded) portion afterwards. Shape and make bottom joints as described below.

6 Alternatively, finials and joints may be cut by hand. In this case, cut upright to indicated shape, then taper to 1¼ in (32mm) square at top, leaving all from arm-joint area down, full size.

7 Mark out finial and top joint (Fig 37) and square lines all round. Saw-cut at these lines and use chisel, gouge or knife to cut to shape. Keep tenon full size and round. Finish with abrasive paper. Try joint tenon in ¾in (19mm) test hole.

8 Mark out and cut bottom tenon in a similar way. It should be long enough to go through thickness of seat.

9 Mark out position of mortice for arm joint. Cut these in any conventional way, ¾in (19mm) long, ½in (12mm) wide, 1in (25mm) deep. Keep mating area of back upright flat and not curved at this point to give a neat, fitting joint.

10 Round over edges of uprights, but keeping arm-joint and bottom-joint areas square for now. Emphasise rounding over on inside front edges (at shoulder level of sitter) for added comfort.

NOTE: Back uprights and arms – and seat when made later – are best marked out from paper or hardboard patterns made by scaling up the squared diagrams.

MAKING AND JOINTING ARMS

11 Cut out arms, as in Fig 37; make a pair, left and right, by reversing pattern. Try to 'bookmatch' the grain figure of the arms.

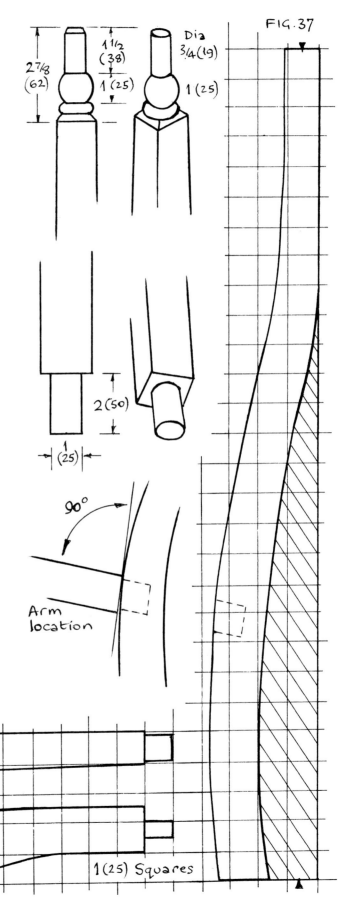

FIG. 37

1 (25) Squares

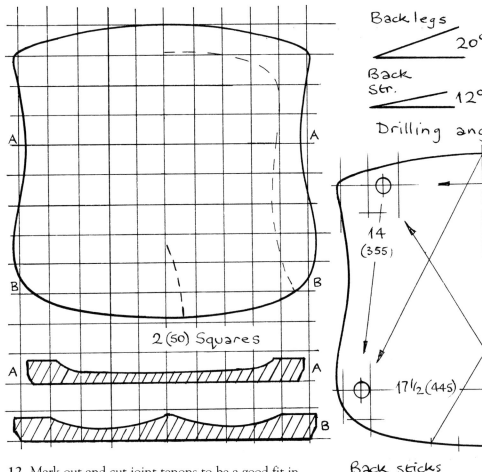

2 (50) Squares

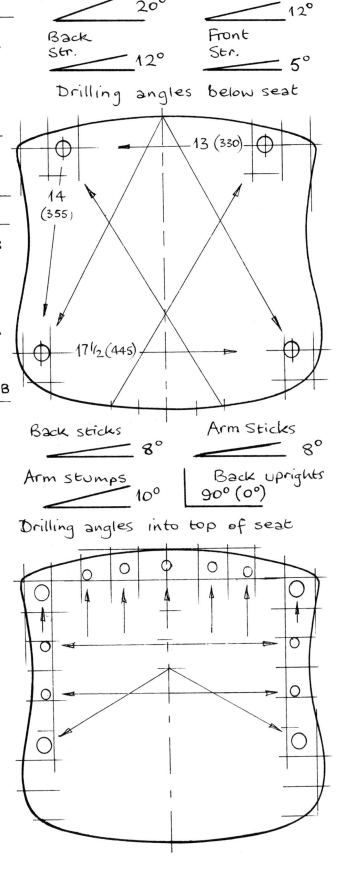

12 Mark out and cut joint tenons to be a good fit in mortices already made in back upright. Note that the tenons are ½in (12mm) thick, conventionally one third the width of the back upright at joint area.

SEAT SHAPING AND DRILLING

13 Cut seat to pattern in Fig 38. Use a single piece of wood if possible, or grain-match and edge-joint separate narrower boards.

14 Mark out area of seat to be hollowed, and rough out to the drawn lines and profiles. Leave final finish until later.

15 Mark out position of leg sockets on underside of seat, and draw in alignment lines. Drill these at required angles, front legs 10°, back legs 20°, all at 1in (25mm) diameter, 1⅛ in (28mm) deep. Take particular care not to drill front-leg sockets too deep.

16 Mark out top component socket positions and alignment lines; back uprights, back- and side-sticks and arm-stumps.

17 Note that back upright sockets go down through the seat (to make a wedged joint) and are drilled vertically, *ie* at 90° to seat surface. Drill 1in (25mm) in diameter.

18 Drill arm-stump sockets 1in (25mm) in diameter, 1¼in (32mm) deep; note that these are at a compound angle of 10°.

19 Drill back- and side-stick sockets, ¾in (19mm) in diameter, 1in (25mm) deep at angle of 8°. The extra depth is a help when assembling.

COMB SHAPING AND DRILLING

20 Cut out the curved shape of the comb (Fig 39). Clean up broad surfaces.

21 Mark out position of back upright and back-stick sockets on lower edge of comb, and drill these before further shaping; back upright sockets ¾in (19mm) in diameter, 1½in (38mm) deep, back-stick sockets ½in (12mm) diameter, ¾in (19mm) deep. Extra depth allows for lateral adjustment of comb at assembly.

22 Mark out and cut top edge of comb to shape; keep lower edge almost square, but round over all other edges to prevent comb looking 'heavy'.

FIG. 39

1 (25) Squares

Marking out the seat for top components

Drilling the seat for top components

Drilling the comb

CUTTING OUT ROCKERS

23 Mark out rockers and cut to shape (Fig 39). Avoid getting a 'flat' on curve at bottom, as this will spoil the rocking movement and comfort.

24 The stated radius of 43in (1,090mm) can be marked using a piece of cord tied to a pencil and held central to the arc. Keep cord tight when marking out the curves. Cut the pair of rockers, one inside the other to minimise waste; dimensions given in cutting list allows for this.

FITTING LEGS AND STRETCHERS

25 With seat upside-down on protected surface, fit legs into seat sockets to full depth and orientate grain figure to best advantage.

26 Mark position of cross-stretchers on each leg (Fig 36). Identify legs, remove and drill stretcher sockets ¾in (19mm) in diameter, 1in (25mm) deep, front legs to angle of 5°, back legs 12°.

27 Replace legs, and check required length of stretchers by measuring across legs, centre to centre. Remember stretchers are intended to stretch legs apart when properly fitted. Adjust stretcher lengths if necessary.

31 Chamfer top edges of rockers, round over fore and aft ends, and lightly round over bottom edges to remove cutting edges.

32 Trial-fit the rockers and check for a smooth rocking action. When satisfied, remove rockers and disassemble underframe from seat ready for a later stage.

DRILLING AND SHAPING ARMS

33 On underside of arms, mark position of arm-stump and back-stick sockets and draw in alignment lines. See Fig 41 which shows a left arm. Reverse for right arm.

34 Drill arm-stump sockets ⅞in (22mm) in diameter, 1in (25mm) deep at compound angle of 15° to allow for upward and outward slope of the arm.

35 Drill arm-stick sockets ½in (12mm) in diameter, ¾in (19mm) deep at angle of 12° and to alignment lines.

36 Shape arms to be 'comfortable'. Leave square at back upright joint areas for now, but round over all edges and front end, emphasising inside top edges of each arm. Carve end-scrolls at this time, or leave plain.

FIG. 40

28 Check stretcher tenons individually into their respective sockets to ensure a fit. Then ease legs out of their sockets, manipulate stretchers into place, and press or tap legs down and stretchers to full depth. Check for stability on a level surface; adjust if necessary.

JOINTING ROCKERS

29 With seat and underframe assembled and standing on a level surface, place rockers alongside legs and mark position for leg-joint sockets (Fig 40). Mark in sight lines as shown.

30 Drill sockets 1in (25mm) in diameter, 1in (25mm) deep, supporting each rocker on a wedge. Line up drill with alignment lines to obtain the necessary compound angle as shown.

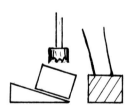

JOINING ARMS AND BACK UPRIGHTS

37 Trial-fit arm-tenons into back upright mortices to obtain a good fit. Then glue these two components together to make two 'sub-units' (Fig 41).

38 Use a sash cramp and soft blocks or pads to apply longitudinal pressure to bring joint shoulders into close contact. Put to one side until set, then complete shaping in joint area.

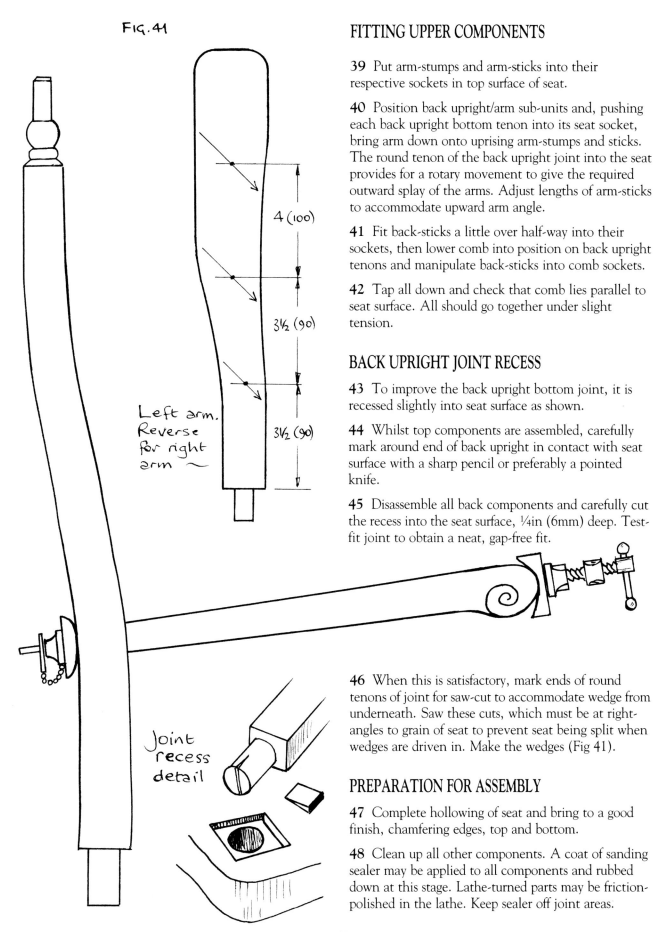

FIG. 41

4 (100)

3½ (90)

Left arm.
Reverse
for right
arm ~

3½ (90)

Joint
recess
detail

FITTING UPPER COMPONENTS

39 Put arm-stumps and arm-sticks into their respective sockets in top surface of seat.

40 Position back upright/arm sub-units and, pushing each back upright bottom tenon into its seat socket, bring arm down onto uprising arm-stumps and sticks. The round tenon of the back upright joint into the seat provides for a rotary movement to give the required outward splay of the arms. Adjust lengths of arm-sticks to accommodate upward arm angle.

41 Fit back-sticks a little over half-way into their sockets, then lower comb into position on back upright tenons and manipulate back-sticks into comb sockets.

42 Tap all down and check that comb lies parallel to seat surface. All should go together under slight tension.

BACK UPRIGHT JOINT RECESS

43 To improve the back upright bottom joint, it is recessed slightly into seat surface as shown.

44 Whilst top components are assembled, carefully mark around end of back upright in contact with seat surface with a sharp pencil or preferably a pointed knife.

45 Disassemble all back components and carefully cut the recess into the seat surface, ¼in (6mm) deep. Test-fit joint to obtain a neat, gap-free fit.

46 When this is satisfactory, mark ends of round tenons of joint for saw-cut to accommodate wedge from underneath. Saw these cuts, which must be at right-angles to grain of seat to prevent seat being split when wedges are driven in. Make the wedges (Fig 41).

PREPARATION FOR ASSEMBLY

47 Complete hollowing of seat and bring to a good finish, chamfering edges, top and bottom.

48 Clean up all other components. A coat of sanding sealer may be applied to all components and rubbed down at this stage. Lathe-turned parts may be friction-polished in the lathe. Keep sealer off joint areas.

ASSEMBLE UNDERFRAME

49 With seat upside-down on a firm but protected surface, put glue into leg sockets in seat and into stretcher sockets in legs.

50 Fit legs part-way into their respective sockets, add stretcher, and push or tap everything into place and joints to full depth.

51 Check on a level surface for stability. Do not fit rockers until later.

ASSEMBLE UPPER COMPONENTS

52 Do each side separately, then add back-sticks and comb.

53 Put glue into arm-stump and arm-stick sockets on one side. Place arm-stump and sticks into place, orientating for best grain figure to front.

54 Put glue into back upright socket and recess, and into underarm sockets. Enter back upright into joint in seat, bringing arm down onto uprising stump and sticks. Press or tap home with a soft mallet.

55 Repeat with opposite side components.

56 Fit wedges in back upright tenons and hammer in tight. Clean off flush later.

57 Put glue into back-stick sockets in seat; fit back-sticks a little over half-way into their sockets and orientate for best grain figure to front.

58 Put glue into comb sockets and bring down onto uprising back upright tenons and back-sticks. Tap down with soft mallet; ensure comb is parallel to seat surface. All should go together under slight tension. Clean off any surplus glue and leave to dry.

FITTING ROCKERS

59 Put glue into sockets in rockers, and fit correct (left or right) rockers onto legs to full depth of joint. Clean off any surplus glue and leave to dry.

FINISHING

60 With a coat of sealer already applied, finish off by wax polishing.

NOTES FOR CHAIR WITHOUT ROCKERS

61 The chair may be made without rockers, but this will require changes to the underframe at stages 25 to 28 to provide an extra pair of stretchers in lieu of the support and strength provided by the rockers.

62 The extra stretchers can be fitted in two ways: (a) by adding side-stretchers to those already provided, to make a box-stretcher arrangement: measure to the mid-line between front and back legs, 1½in (38mm) below the existing cross-stretcher socket positions, and make two stretchers to this length.

63 Drill sockets at these points at right-angles (90°) to previously drilled sockets. Use the short dowel method (see page 76) to ensure the correct angle. Drilling angles will be 8° front legs, 14° back legs.

64 Assemble underframe as described (Fig 42).

65 (b) An alternative method is, at stages 25 to 28, to fit stretchers between front and back legs (*ie* side-stretchers instead of cross-stretchers) and to fit a centre cross-stretcher to make an 'H' stretcher arrangement.

66 Mark socket positions as described at stage 26, but orientate to face fore and aft. Drill sockets at these points. Measure required length of stretchers.

67 Make stretchers and trial-fit these to legs.

68 Whilst assembled, ascertain position and length of centre cross-stretcher.

69 Make centre cross-stretcher and drill the marked sockets.

70 Assemble underframe as described (Fig 42).

Detail of the wedged joint of back upright into the seat

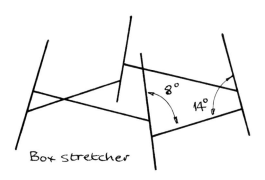

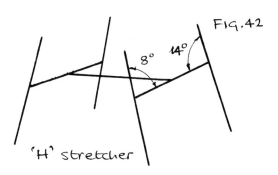

Box stretcher   'H' stretcher   FIG. 42

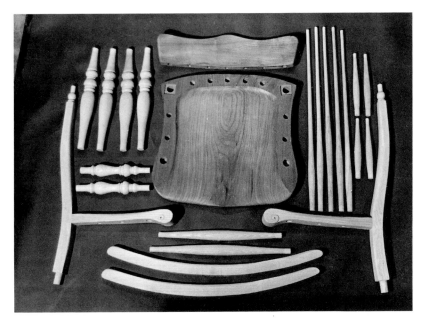

Rocking chair parts

ROCKING CHAIR		CUTTING LIST (Add waste)	
No.	ITEM	INCHES	mm
1	Seat	21 × 20 × 1¾	530 × 510 × 44
4	Legs	16 × 2 × 2	410 × 50 × 50
2	Stretchers	20 × 1½ × 1½	510 × 38 × 38
1	(for 2 uprights)	28 × 6 × 1½	710 × 150 × 38
2	Arms	16 × 2½ × 2	410 × 62 × 50
2	Arm-stumps	11 × 1⅞ × 1⅞	280 × 47 × 47
5	Back-sticks	28 × 1 × 1	710 × 25 × 25
4	Side-sticks	10 × 1 × 1	255 × 25 × 25
1	(for comb)	20 × 5 × 2¼	510 × 125 × 56
1	(for 2 rockers)	30 × 5 × 1½	760 × 125 × 38

GIMSON LADDERBACK

This style of chair is named after Ernest Gimson (1864-1919), an architect by training who, under the influence of William Morris, turned his attentions to the wider design pursuits and hand craftsmanship of the Arts and Crafts Movement. During the early 1880s he became acquainted with the brothers Ernest and Sidney Barnsley, and for some years the three worked together in a rural Cotswold idyll designing and making furniture and such like, and carrying out architectural commissions.

In about 1887 or 1888 Gimson, having seen some rush-seated chairs made by Philip Clissett (page 88), sought out the maker and spent some time with him learning the basic skills of the chairmaker's craft. Subsequently Gimson made, or had made, rush-seated ladderback chairs to his own design, and these are still being produced today.

This freely interpreted design is characterised by the high back and multiple ladders typical of the Gimson style. A somewhat more refined chair than the earlier Clissett, it still retains an essentially rural appearance, due largely to its basically similar method of construction and use of materials. This structural simplicity is reflected in the five relatively unsophisticated back-slats which decrease in width from top to bottom.

The shape and arrangement of back-slats in ladderback chairs has been shown to be an important 'stylistic signature', a means of identifying chairs from different regions and even from individual makers. The shape and arrangement of back-slats in this chair is, of course, open to individual interpretations; those shown and described here are simply my own choice.

As is to be expected, the basic method of construction has much in common with the Clissett armchair already described (pages 88–95), and to avoid too much repetition some working references are made back to that section.

Made throughout in ash, the completed chair was dark stained and finally wax polished.

Ladderback chair by Ernest Gimson, c1899

114

RECIPE

TURNED COMPONENTS

1 Turn, or round, the two back uprights, 45in (1,140mm) long, 1½in (38mm) in diameter. Taper slightly at ends.

2 Turn or round the two front uprights, 28in (710mm) long, 1½in (38mm) in diameter. Taper slightly. Refer to Fig 43.

3 Turn or round the seven stretchers of the underframe; two front ones at 19in (480mm) long, and five others at 17½in (445mm) long; all 1in (25mm) in diameter. These last will be adjusted to their correct lengths later. All stretchers taper to ⅝in (16mm) joints.

4 Seat-rails may also be turned, but should be cleft as described on page 74. Make three 16in (410mm) long; one 19in (480mm) long, with ⅝in (16mm) joints.

BACK-SLATS

5 Cut material for the five back-slats. For now, keep them rectangular and of equal width to simplify bending. Fig 43.

BENDING BACK UPRIGHTS AND SLATS

6 Follow instructions given for bending on page 36.

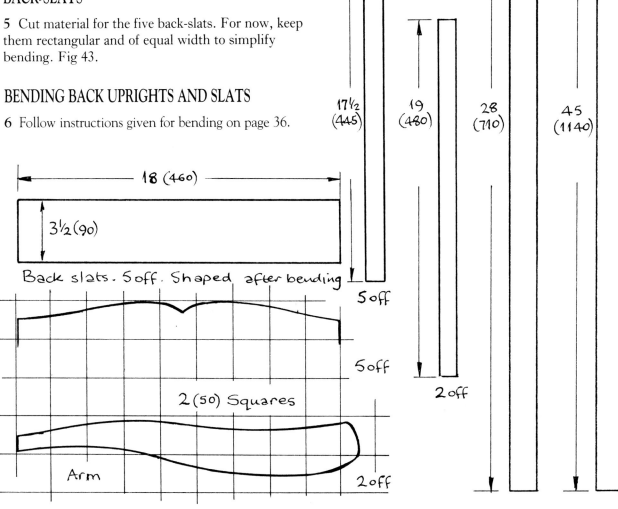

FIG. 43

All rail and stretcher joints are ⅝ (16)

16 (410)   19 (480)

3 off   1 off   2 off

17½ (445)   19 (480)   28 (710)   45 (1140)

18 (460)

3½ (90)

Back slats. 5 off. Shaped after bending

5 off   5 off   2 off

2 (50) Squares

Arm   2 off

7 Use formers used for previous ladderback chairs (described on page 75).

CUTTING AND SHAPING ARMS

8 Cut to pattern in Fig 43. Make a pair, left and right.

9 First, taper back ends and round to a ⅝in (16mm) joint to fit back upright. Then shape and smooth arms until you have a comfortable feel and appearance. Keep front end full for jointing. See note on page 91.

MARKING OUT AND DRILLING UPRIGHTS (I)

10 When back uprights are dry, remove from former; placed on a level surface the uprights will lie naturally flat. On a centre line, mark out position of *across* socket positions for seat-rail and stretchers (Fig 44).

11 Front uprights should be held in a 'V' cradle. Orientate for best grain figure to front, then mark 'inside' surfaces for seat-rail and stretcher socket positions.

12 Drill these sockets, all ⅝in (16mm) diameter, ⅞in (22mm) deep. Use the sliding 'V' cradle (page 27) for consistent alignment of sockets, or use the short dowel method (pages 76 and 77).

FIRST TRIAL FIT

13 Reduce back stretcher to 16in (410mm) and check that all other across-stretchers and rails are of correct length. Try these individually for fit.

14 Then make two separate sections, a back 'ladder' and a front 'ladder'. Place on a flat surface and check for wind. Adjust by gentle twisting if necessary.

socket and using an angle-finder device (see page 27) to set correct angle (Fig 44).

being greater than 90°, angle outward; side sockets into front uprights, being less than 90°, angle inward. Take extra care when marking out and drilling.

MARKING OUT AND DRILLING UPRIGHTS (II)

15 Whilst still assembled, mark out on centre line position of side-rail and stretcher sockets. Refer to Fig 45 on page 118. Disassemble for drilling.

16 Because the chair is wider at the front than at the back, these sockets must be drilled at an angle. The 6° drilling angle is obtained by placing a short length of tight-fitting ⅝in (16mm) dowel in a previously drilled

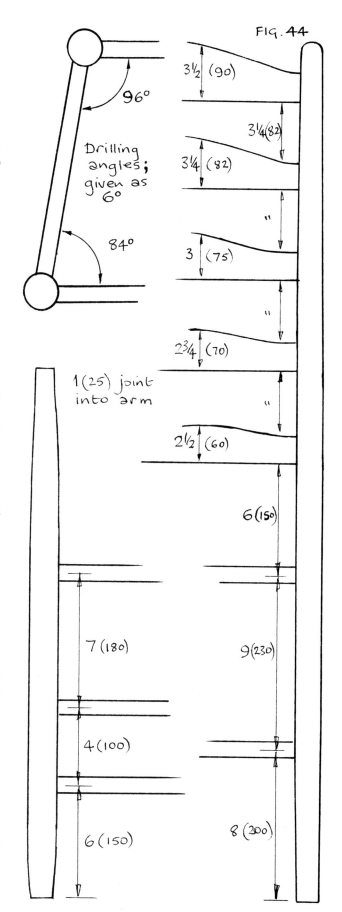

FIG. 44

socket and using an angle-finder device (see page 27) to set correct angle (Fig 44).

17 Support arch of back uprights when drilling.

18 Sockets for arms should be drilled at this time also. Drill these with top portion of back upright held horizontal, to give slight upward and outward angle when chair is assembled. Drill ⅝in (16mm) in diameter, ⅞in (22mm) deep.

SECOND TRIAL FIT

19 Assemble back and front ladders again.

20 Then add side seat-rails and stretchers. They should spring in under slight tension. Make sure all joints go to full depth.

21 Stand on a level surface and check for stability. Correct by gently twisting if necessary.

MEASURING AND FITTING ARMS

22 With chair-frame assembled so far, trial-fit arms into their respective sockets in back uprights. Ensure that they go to full depth. Allow arm to lie on top, or to one side of uprising front upright, and mark position for joint socket in underside of each arm. Offset this measurement very slightly forwards to ensure a tension fit and to help keep the back tenon tight into the back upright socket.

23 Remove arms and drill sockets at marked places, 1in (25mm) in diameter, 1in (25mm) deep. Do this with great care. Because the arms angle upwards, it is necessary to drill at an angle of 8°. Fig 29 on page 94 shows a method of doing this. Note the end tenon is highest when drilling, and remember you are drilling left and right arms.

24 Try arms for good fit and comfortable feel, and when satisfied, go on to next stage.

MEASURING AND CUTTING BACK-SLATS

25 With chair-frame still assembled, correct length of back-slats can be measured. Check that joints are still fully 'home', then measure across between mid-line of each back upright.

26 Cut back-slats to length; be generous, and trim to size when fitting if necessary.

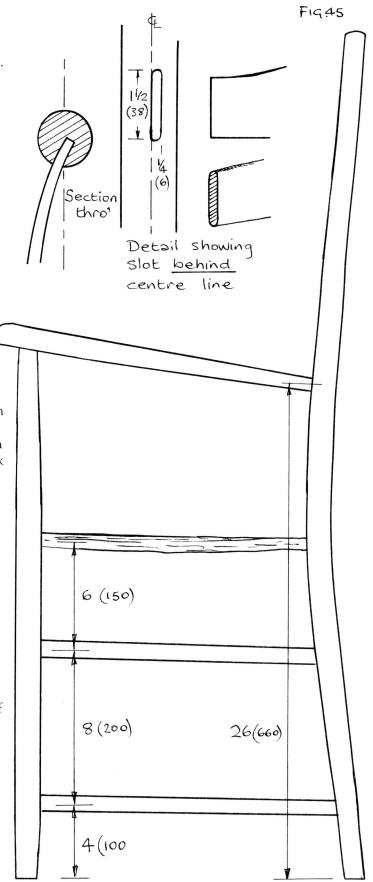

FIG 45

1½ (38)

¼ (6)

Section thro'

Detail showing slot behind centre line

6 (150)

8 (200)

26 (660)

4 (100

MARKING AND CUTTING BACK-SLAT MORTICES

27 With chair-frame disassembled, lay each back upright on level surface, inner faces upwards. Mark position of each mortice slot to *back* of centre line on each upright. Refer to Fig 45 and note on page 76.

28 Cut these mortices by any available means, as previously described.

29 For accuracy and alignment use a sliding 'V' cradle (page 27). Keep ends of slots rounded to suit rounded edges of slats. Slots are all one size, 1½in (38mm) long, ¼in (6mm) wide, ¾in (19mm) deep.

SHAPING AND FITTING BACK-SLATS

30 Cut slats to their separate widths, and mark out the curved top edge to the shape given in Fig 43. Make a paper or card pattern from this, and use it as a basic guide to draw the outline of each slat. Ensure that ends are kept a little over 1½in (38mm) wide for trimming to fit.

31 Shape slats to pattern, then trim, rounding their edges, and fit individually.

32 Note that slats increase in width upwards (Fig 44).

33 When each slat fits individually, assemble complete back section, including slats, and check on level surface for wind. Correct if necessary.

FINAL TRIAL FIT

34 Complete assembly of chair-frame by making front 'ladder' and adding side-rails and stretchers. Check all joints go to full depth, and test on a level surface for stability. When satisfied, disassemble.

PREPARATION FOR ASSEMBLY

35 Clean up all components and remove any unwanted marks.

36 If the chair is to be left with a natural finish, sanding sealer may be applied at this stage (see page 41). Keep off joint areas.

FINAL ASSEMBLY

37 Follow assembly in sequence as already described.

38 Put glue in correct sockets and slot mortices in

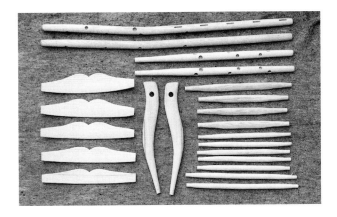

Gimson ladderback chair parts

back uprights; fit stretcher, rail and slats and push fully home. Check on a level surface.

39 Put glue in correct sockets in front uprights; fit stretchers and rail, and push fully home. Check on a level surface.

40 Put glue in remaining sockets (except arm-joint socket), fit remaining components and push all fully home. Stand on a level surface and check stability.

41 Fit arms by first putting glue into sockets; enter end ⅝in (16mm) joints fully into place, and bring each arm down onto its respective front upright. Tap down if necessary.

42 Check chair again for stability, and correct if required. Clean off any surplus glue, and leave to dry.

FINISHING

43 The chair described was given a dark stain before its seat was woven; it was then wax polished. See page 42 for finishing details.

GIMSON LADDERBACK CUTTING LIST (Add waste)			
No.	ITEM	INCHES	mm
2	Back uprights	45 × 1½ × 1½	1140 × 38 × 38
2	Front uprights	28 × 1½ × 1½	710 × 38 × 38
1	Seat-rail (cleft)	19 × 1½ × 1	480 × 38 × 25
3	Seat-rails (cleft)	16 × 1½ × 1	410 × 38 × 25
2	Stretchers	19 × 1 × 1	480 × 25 × 25
5	Stretchers	17½ × 1 × 1	445 × 25 × 25
5	Back-slats	18 × 3½ × ⅜	460 × 90 × 9
2	Arms	19 × 3 × 1½	480 × 75 × 38

SPINDLEBACK

This chair is a further representative of the simple open frame construction, though the ones so far depicted have been made with curved slats across the back, to make the chair type known as 'ladderback'. However, a common alternative to back 'ladders' was to use rails across the back, between which were fitted turned spindles; this feature gave rise to the name 'spindleback' to describe this type of chair.

The spindleback chair was especially popular in the West Midlands and north-western counties of England where it was made in several forms, often with features peculiar to a specific area of that wide region. The earliest examples, from around the late eighteenth century, had only one row of spindles but later, in parts of Cheshire and Lancashire, chairs with two and sometimes three rows of spindles predominated and became characteristic of these areas.

Most of the northern spindlebacks had rush seats, though in the West Midlands the majority were of a style peculiar to that region. These consisted of a panel of wood chamfered at its edges, which slotted into a groove made into round seat-rails at sides and back, and supported at the front on a flat apron rail. It is this type of chair which is described here: with its single row of turned spindles and inset wooden panel seat, it offers both an alternative back arrangement and a different form of seat provision.

The original chairs would have been sturdily made to withstand the hard usage which they were likely to receive, and the style would have been as familiar in farmhouse and cottage as it became in the houses and workplaces of the industrial towns. The chair-frame was made in ash, and the seat in elm; on completion, it was finished with a light stain and wax polished.

Spindleback chair

RECIPE

FIG. 46

MAKING TURNED COMPONENTS

1 Lathe-turn, or otherwise round, two back uprights and two front uprights, both 2in (50mm) in diameter, 40in (1,020mm) and 19in (480mm) in length respectively. Front uprights may be turned to pattern in Fig 46 or left plain. Give slight taper to lower end and to top of back uprights. Keep full size at seat-rail level. Back uprights are to be bent (see below).

2 Make three seat-rails, 1¼in (32mm) in diameter, 16½in (420mm) long.

3 Make two stretchers for front, 1in (25mm) in diameter, 19in (480mm) long. Make six stretchers and three top rails, 1in (25mm) in diameter, 17½in (445mm) long. Two stretchers (for back) will require shortening later to 16½in (420mm) long; the three top rails will be bent.

4 Lathe-turn the four back spindles.

BENDING BACK UPRIGHTS AND TOP RAILS

5 Follow instructions given for bending on page 36.

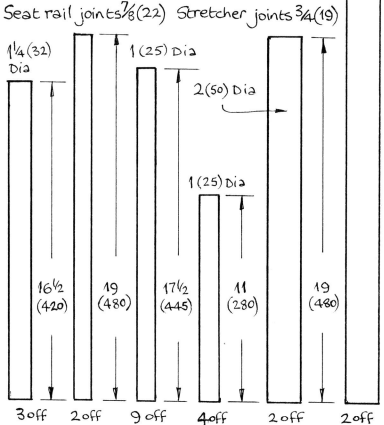

Seat rail joints ⅞ (22)   Stretcher joints ¾ (19)

1¼ (32) Dia   1 (25) Dia   2 (50) Dia   1 (25) Dia

16½ (420)   19 (480)   17½ (445)   11 (280)   19 (480)

3 off   2 off   9 off   4 off   2 off   2 off

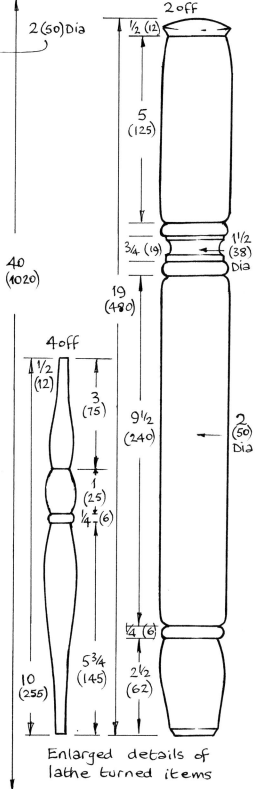

2 (50) Dia

40 (1020)

2 off

½ (12)

5 (125)

¾ (19)   1½ (38) Dia

19 (480)

9½ (240)

2 (50) Dia

¼ (6)

2½ (62)

4 off

½ (12)

3 (75)

1 (25)

¼ (6)

10 (255)

5¾ (145)

Enlarged details of lathe turned items

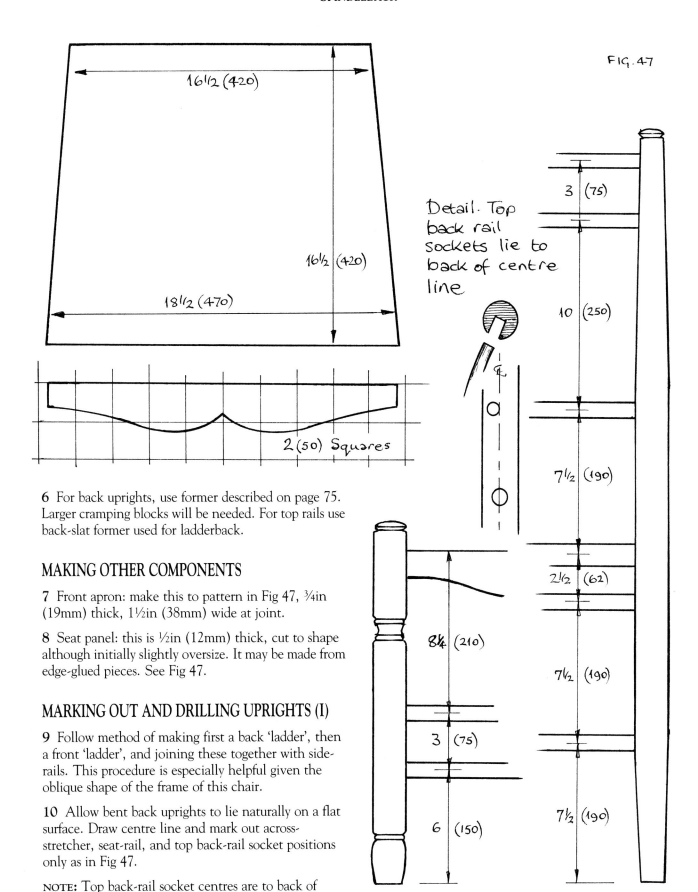

FIG. 47

16½ (420)

16½ (420)

18½ (470)

2 (50) Squares

Detail. Top back rail sockets lie to back of centre line

3 (75)

10 (250)

7½ (190)

2½ (62)

7½ (190)

8¼ (210)

3 (75)

6 (150)

7½ (190)

6 For back uprights, use former described on page 75. Larger cramping blocks will be needed. For top rails use back-slat former used for ladderback.

MAKING OTHER COMPONENTS

7 Front apron: make this to pattern in Fig 47, ¾in (19mm) thick, 1½in (38mm) wide at joint.

8 Seat panel: this is ½in (12mm) thick, cut to shape although initially slightly oversize. It may be made from edge-glued pieces. See Fig 47.

MARKING OUT AND DRILLING UPRIGHTS (I)

9 Follow method of making first a back 'ladder', then a front 'ladder', and joining these together with side-rails. This procedure is especially helpful given the oblique shape of the frame of this chair.

10 Allow bent back uprights to lie naturally on a flat surface. Draw centre line and mark out across-stretcher, seat-rail, and top back-rail socket positions only as in Fig 47.

NOTE: Top back-rail socket centres are to back of centre line to allow for their curvature.

11 Draw centre line on front uprights and mark

positions of across-stretcher sockets. Mark all uprights as left or right.

12 Using the 'V' cradle, drill these sockets; stretcher and top-rail sockets ¾in (19mm) in diameter, 1in (25mm) deep, the back seat-rail socket ⅞in (22mm) in diameter, ⅞in (22mm) deep. Align sockets using

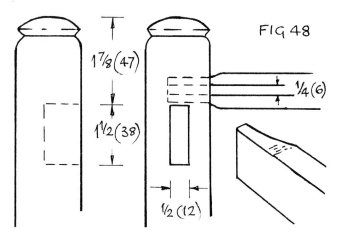

FIG 48

short dowel method, or use the sliding 'V' cradle. See page 27.

13 Mark out position of front apron mortices carefully so they line up with the slots which will be made in the side (and back) seat-rails to accommodate the seat panel (Fig 48).

FITTING FRONT APRON

14 Cut the front apron mortices as marked in both front uprights; use chain-drilling method followed by careful chiselling. Keep end of mortices square, 1½in (38mm) long, ½in (12mm) wide, ¾in (19mm) deep.

15 Taper and trim apron tenons; the taper gives a tight joint and neat appearance to front (Fig 48).

FIRST TRIAL ASSEMBLY

16 Check that rails and stretchers are of correct length. Shorten the two back stretchers to 16½in (420mm); the two front stretchers are 19in (480mm). Check that individual joints go to full depth.

17 Join pairs of uprights to make front and back ladders. Include the bent top rails; adjust the length of these if necessary.

18 Place on a flat surface and check for wind; correct by gentle twisting if needed.

MARKING OUT AND DRILLING UPRIGHTS (II)

19 With two ladders still assembled and on a flat

surface, mark position of side seat-rail and stretcher socket positions.

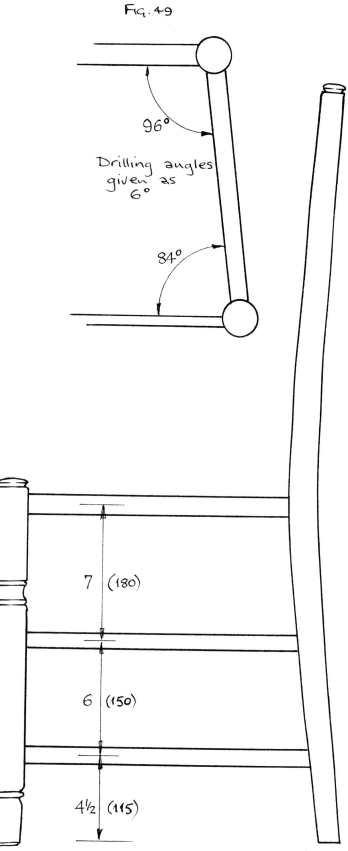

FIG. 49

96°

Drilling angles given as 6°

84°

20 Check that seat-rail sockets in back uprights are level with each other so that seat-panel slots (when made) are in line. This means it will be necessary to mitre end of each tenon to obtain a good fit. Note also relative position of side seat-rails to front apron in front uprights. Seat panel (when fitted) overlies the apron (Fig 50).

21 Drill these sockets, seat-rail sockets ⅞in (22mm) in diameter, ⅞in (22mm) deep; stretcher sockets, ¾in (19mm) in diameter, 1in (25mm) deep. Obtain the required 6° angle by placing a short length of tight-fitting ¾in (19mm) dowel in a previously drilled socket, and use an angle-finder device (see page 27) to set correct angle (Fig 49).

22 Support arch of back upright when applying drilling pressure to avoid risk of breakage.

NOTE: The oblique shape of the chair-frame, giving a seat shape which is wider at the front than at the back, requires care when marking out and drilling: side sockets in back uprights angle outwards, ie are greater than 90°; side sockets in front uprights angle inwards ie are less than 90°. The actual drilling angle in each case is given as 6° (see Fig 49).

SIDE-RAILS AND STRETCHERS

23 Curve of back uprights means side-stretcher lengths will vary. Side seat-rails are correct length, 16½in (420mm) long. Ascertain correct stretcher lengths, as described on page 76. Check that individual joints fit satisfactorily.

SECOND TRIAL ASSEMBLY

24 Assemble back and front ladders. Join these together with side-rails and stretchers. Make sure all joints go to full depth. Stand on level surface and check for wobble; adjust by gentle twisting if needed.

SEAT PANEL FITTING

25 The seat panel is housed in slots in the seat-rails and overlies the front apron. The slots or grooves may be made by any suitable means, by hand or machine; I made a simple box jig to hold rail, and used a router. The slots are ¼in (6mm) wide, ⅜in (9mm) deep. See Fig 50.

Trial assembly prior to gluing up

125

26 With chair-frame assembled, check exact measurement for seat panel (it may differ from dimensions given).

27 Trim panel to size, chamfer underside edges to fit snug in slots; overlap front apron, ½in (12mm). Trim corners to fit neatly around uprights (Fig 50). Trial-fit until satisfactory. Round over front top edge.

FITTING BACK SPINDLES

28 Mark position of the four back spindles on two curved top rails (Fig 51); it is advisable to do this with the curved rails in position. Measure space between the two back uprights and divide this equally. Treat the measurements given as a guide only.

29 Drill these carefully, ½in (12mm) in diameter, ½in (12mm) deep. Try spindles for good fit. Keep this 'sub-unit' together and trial-fit between back uprights.

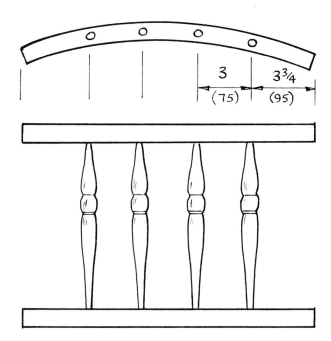

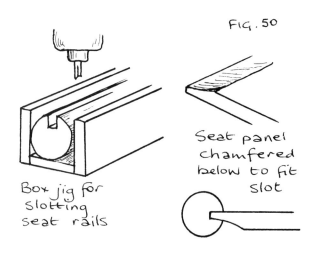

FIG. 50

Box jig for slotting seat rails

Seat panel chamfered below to fit slot

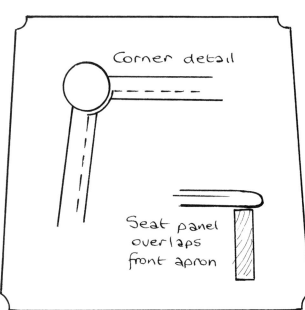

Corner detail

Seat panel overlaps front apron

FINAL ASSEMBLY

30 Clean up, and clean off any unwanted marks. Assemble in correct sequence.

31 Begin by gluing back spindles into top rails.

32 Then assemble back ladder; glue into sockets, insert spindles 'sub-unit' and all other components to full depth. Check for wind.

33 Now, glue into sockets and assemble front ladder. Check for wind.

34 Finally add side-rails and stretchers, not forgetting to include the seat panel at this stage. Put glue into sockets but not into seat slots – these are left dry to allow for any movement of the seat panel. Stand on a level surface and check for stability. Wipe off surplus glue and leave to dry.

FINISHING

35 The chair was given a light stain, followed by sealing, and finally wax polishing. See page 42.

Final assembly of the chair

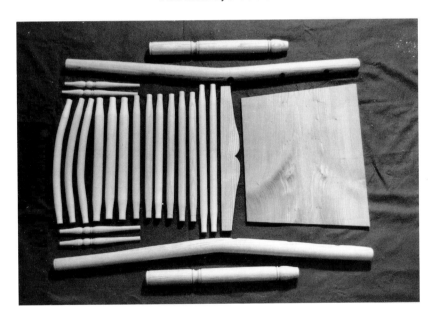

Spindleback chair parts

SPINDLEBACK		CUTTING LIST (Add waste)		
No.	ITEM	INCHES		mm
2	Back uprights	40 × 2 × 2		1020 × 50 × 50
2	Front legs	19 × 2 × 2		480 × 50 × 50
3	Seat-rails	16½ × 1¼ × 1¼		420 × 32 × 32
1	Front apron	19 × 2½ × ¾		480 × 62 × 19
2	Stretchers	19 × 1 × 1		480 × 25 × 25
6	Stretchers	17½ × 1 × 1		445 × 25 × 25
3	Top rails	17½ × 1 × 1		445 × 25 × 25
4	Back spindles	11 × 1 × 1		280 × 25 × 25
1	Seat panel	19 × 17 × ½		480 × 430 × 12

SMOKER'S BOW

This low back style of Windsor chair dates from the early ninetenth century, but its origins go back much further. Several early Welsh, West Country, North of England and Irish chair styles are likely prototypes (the low bow-back, page 80, is an example), while some writers have suggested developmental links with both eighteenth-century Queen Anne elbow chairs and the Philadelphia low back, popular in America from around 1725.

The chair is characterised firstly by its three-part arm-bow consisting of two outward-curving arm sections, bridged and strengthened by a raised and shaped centre-back scroll; and also by its generous turned components and its generally sturdy construction. In fact the style became one of the most popular for use in public places and offices, as well as for domestic purposes. Its usual designation, 'smoker's bow', perhaps refers to its use in the smoking rooms of men's clubs and in public houses; in some areas it was more commonly known as the 'office chair', while in more recent times it is sometimes called a 'broad-arm Windsor'. Some call it a 'barber's chair', while around the coast of Ireland, where it was apparently issued as standard equipment in lighthouses, it is known locally as the 'lighthouse keeper's chair'.

The low back style also appears in other forms and under other names, often confused. Typical amongst these are first, the so-called 'firehouse Windsor', a type used in America during the nineteenth century by volunteer fire companies; and second, the 'captain's chair', said to have been popular in the pilot houses of Mississippi steamboats. The firehouse varient features a box stretcher (whereas the true smoker's bow has a double 'H' arrangement), a cut-out hand-grip in the back scroll, and a less flared arm-bow; while the captain's chair, also usually having a box stretcher, is identifiable by its lighter arm-bow, which is a single bent piece curved downwards at the front where it sockets into the seat. Often these are, arguably, not true Windsors, having framed seats with punched plywood inserts. Essentially American, these two styles are outclassed by yet another close relative, the very English bergère bow with its curvacious back and deeply scrolled arms, a product of Victorian flamboyance.

The smoker's bow, typically made with elm seat and arm-bow, with beech, ash or yew turnings, has enjoyed a wide popularity, both rural and urban, right up to the present time. Minor regional differences occur in those seen today, and the chair made here, with its inverted cup turnings on bulbous legs, is similar to the popular High Wycombe style.

The chair was made with burr elm for the seat and arm-bow; the turned components in yew came from Sussex trees which fell victim to the 1987 autumn hurricane.

A smoker's bow chair from a nineteenth-century catalogue

Recipe

MARKING OUT AND CUTTING ARM BACK-BOW

1 Make patterns of arm parts (Fig 52) and lay out on a planed board; orientate for grain direction, as shown.

2 Cut to shape by hand or on a bandsaw. Make a left and a right arm.

3 Mark out and cut the back scroll to size. This may be built up if necessary and partially shaped at this stage if required. Plane lower face to be a good fit to arms.

MAKING THE ARM BACK-BOW

4 This is built up from the three components: the left and right arms, and the back scroll. The finished shape is achieved after these three separate parts have been joined together. Mating surfaces of each should be flat to ensure a close fit.

5 Accurate assembly is assisted by use of a full-size paper pattern sheet (Fig 52): lay the parts out on this to check shape and jointing. Pay particular attention to the central junction between the two arms, and aim for a neat, close-fitting butt joint. The scroll lies centrally over this, where it is secured by glue and screws.

6 Mark out, drill and counterbore screw-holes in arm pieces as shown in Fig 52. These are strategically positioned so that they avoid spindle sockets drilled later.

7 Locate position of screw-holes on underside of scroll, and drill appropriate pilot-holes in scroll.

8 After a 'dry-run', using screws only to check fit, coat mating surfaces with glue – not forgetting the central butt joint of the two arms – place parts together and screw up tightly. Plug screw-holes, wipe off surplus glue and leave to dry.

SHAPING ARM BACK-BOW

9 Bring arm back-bow to final shape using spokeshaves or other means, and finish with scraper and glasspaper. 'Marry' arms and scroll together, and round everything over to a comfortable shape. Keep lower surface quite flat to accommodate seat spindles and arm-stumps later.

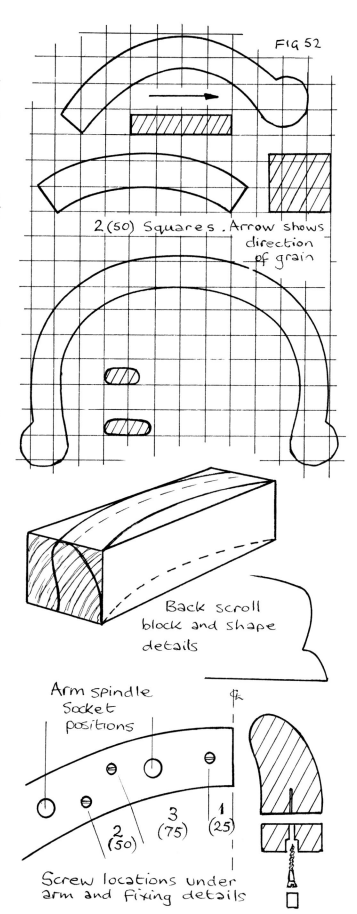

FIG 52

2 (50) Squares. Arrow shows direction of grain

Back scroll block and shape details

Arm spindle socket positions

2 (50)   3 (75)   1 (25)

Screw locations under arm and fixing details

130

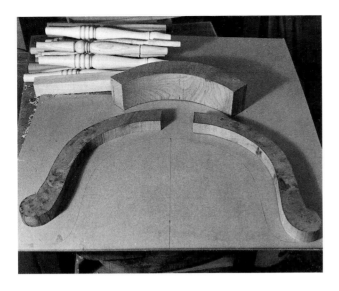

Parts of the arm-bow set out on full size pattern

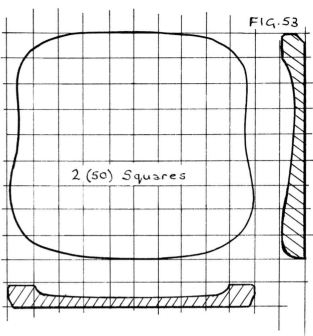

The back scroll partly shaped, ready for gluing

CUTTING AND ROUGH-SHAPING SEAT

10 Cut seat to pattern (Fig 53) by hand or on a bandsaw. The choice of grain direction is entirely arbitrary.

11 Begin hollowing seat to cross-sections shown. Any safe method can be used to remove bulk of waste (see page 34). Pay particular attention to the front edge which should be nicely rounded over, but keep quite substantial at corners where leg sockets will come.

MARKING OUT AND DRILLING SEAT: UNDERSIDE

12 Mark out leg-socket positions on underside of seat, using measurements from Fig 54. Mark in alignment or sight lines.

13 Using the sloping platform and a pillar drill, or any other means, drill the two back leg sockets, 1in (25mm) in diameter and 1¼in (32mm) deep at 20°, and then the front leg sockets, 1in (25mm) diameter and 1⅛in (28mm) deep at 12°. Take care not to drill too deep, especially the front sockets.

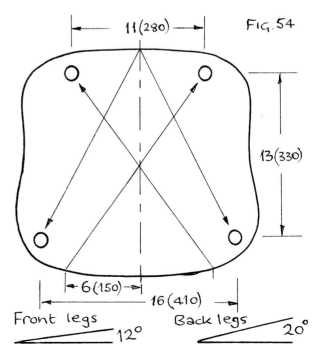

FIG.55

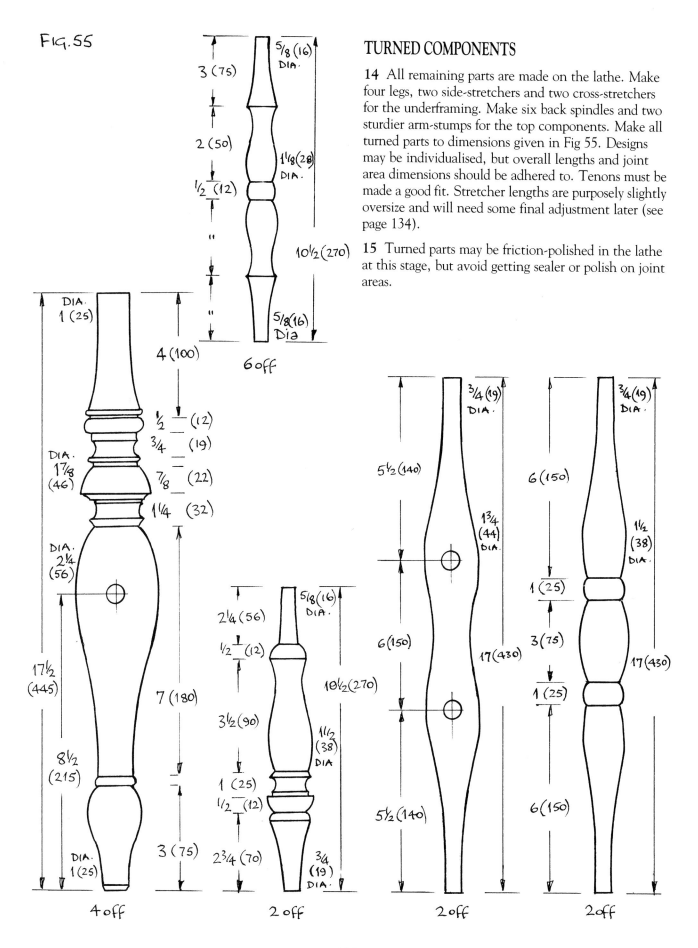

TURNED COMPONENTS

14 All remaining parts are made on the lathe. Make four legs, two side-stretchers and two cross-stretchers for the underframing. Make six back spindles and two sturdier arm-stumps for the top components. Make all turned parts to dimensions given in Fig 55. Designs may be individualised, but overall lengths and joint area dimensions should be adhered to. Tenons must be made a good fit. Stretcher lengths are purposely slightly oversize and will need some final adjustment later (see page 134).

15 Turned parts may be friction-polished in the lathe at this stage, but avoid getting sealer or polish on joint areas.

MARKING OUT AND DRILLING SEAT: TOP

16 Mark out top surface of seat as in Fig 56 to give position of seat-spindle and arm-stump sockets. Spindle sockets are ⅝in (16mm) diameter, 1in (25mm) deep; arm-stump sockets (the two at the front) ¾in (19mm) diameter, 1in (25mm) deep, at angles given.

17 Alignment lines are marked in according to the diagram (Fig 56), radiating from the centre point of the seat.

18 Drill socket-holes at given angles.

MARKING OUT AND DRILLING UNDERSIDE OF ARM-BOW

19 Mark out underside of arm back-bow as in Fig 56 to accommodate the components rising from the seat. To check the accuracy of marked positions, put arm-spindles and stumps into their respective sockets in seat, and place arm back-bow on top ends of uprising components. Compare position with marked places. Make any necessary adjustments at this stage.

20 Mark in alignment lines on underside of arm back-bow. The full-size paper pattern sheet can help in this task – lay out alignment lines on the sheet, and with the arm back-bow in position, continue the lines onto the bow (see Fig 56).

21 Because arm-bow is drilled on its underside, drilling alignment is now reverse of seat-socket drilling to give correct angle orientation.

22 Drill sockets, all ⅝in (16mm) in diameter, ¾in (19mm) deep, at appropriate angles as given in Fig 56.

TRIAL FIT OF UPPER COMPONENTS

23 With arm-spindles and stumps in position in seat, bring arm back-bow down onto them and manipulate end tenons into their respective sockets. See Fig 56. Bow should lie parallel to seat surface and be approximately 10in (255mm) above it. Make any necessary adjustments, and when satisfied, identify component positions and disassemble.

NOTE: Fitting the arm back-bow correctly requires some attention to accurate measurement and joint sizing. The extra depth of the sockets in the seat allows for any adjustment necessary to bring arm back-bow parallel to seat surface.

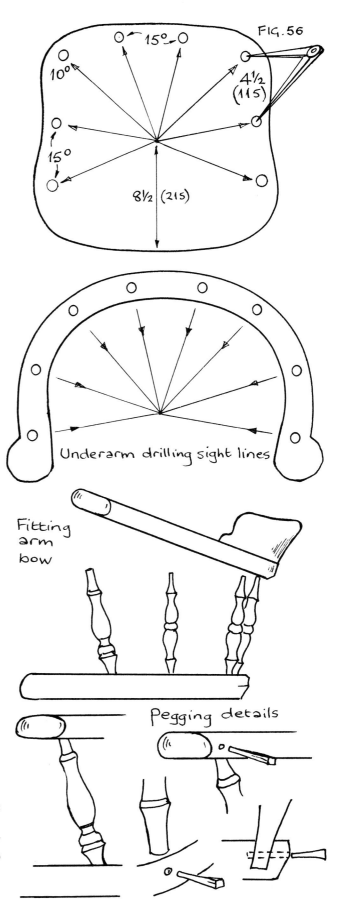

FIG. 56

Underarm drilling sight lines

Fitting arm bow

Pegging details

FITTING LEGS AND STRETCHERS

24 With seat upside-down on bench, check that legs fit securely and fully into sockets previously drilled. Align so that best grain-figure faces forwards, and mark position of side-stretcher sockets on 'inside' surface of each leg. Number legs and appropriate sockets in seat for identification purposes before removing legs – the difference in angles of stretcher sockets do not allow front and back legs to be interchanged.

25 Drill each leg at marked positions, each ¾in (19mm) in diameter and ⅞in (22mm) deep, at appropriate angles as given in Fig 57. The difference in angle between leg sockets and stretcher sockets is because of the compound angle of the former. Use the 'V' cradle, and tilt to correct angle. Leg joint should be highest when drilling stretcher sockets.

26 Join front and back legs with their respective stretchers, and check for fit in seat sockets; adjust stretcher length if necessary (but see note below).

27 With legs and side-stretchers in place, ascertain position, drilling angle and required length of the two cross-stretchers. Do this by placing cross-stretchers across side-stretchers, and measure and mark. Spread legs outwards and sideways whilst doing this. Note that slight narrowing of side-stretchers, front to back, requires sockets drilled at slight angle of 5°.

28 Disassemble, drill side-stretchers as required, and reassemble. Make any necessary adjustments and when satisfied, disassemble.

NOTE: Remember that stretchers should stretch legs apart, giving the required amount of tension to the chair. Too much tension and the chair will be difficult, if not impossible, to assemble; too little (components too loose) and the chair will not be truly well made. It is a matter of getting it just right.

The final clean up before assembly

FINAL SHAPING AND CLEANING UP

29 Complete work on seat. Clean up and smooth hollowed area; clean up side edge all around, working a light bevel on top edge and a larger one on bottom edge, as in Fig 57, to take away some of the visual weight of the seat.

30 Clean up and smooth arm back-bow. If turned components were not friction-polished, clean these up also. A coat of sanding sealer can be applied to all components not previously polished, avoiding joint areas.

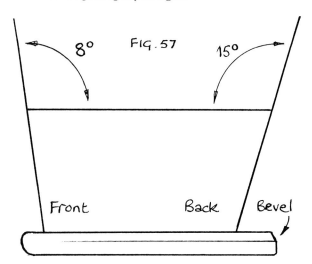

Assembling top components

134

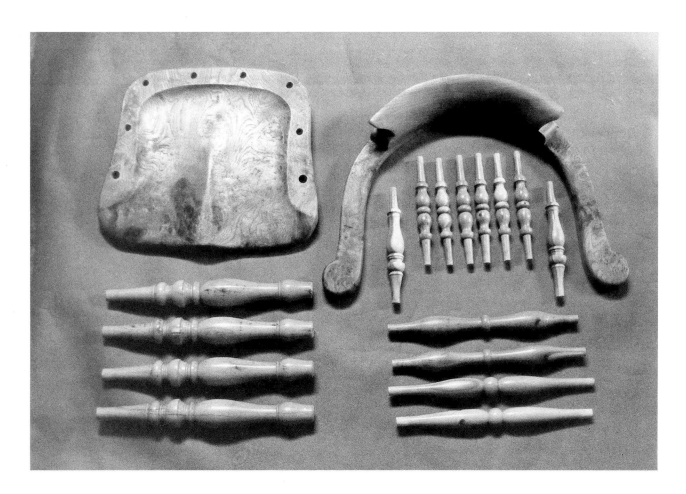

Smoker's bow chair parts

FINAL ASSEMBLY: UNDERFRAME

31 With seat upside-down on protected bench, put glue into all socket-holes; insert cross-stretchers into side-stretcher sockets, place legs just into the seat sockets, and add stretchers. Push all into place, using a soft mallet to persuade tight joints to their full depth. Stand chair on a flat surface and check no rocking.

FINAL ASSEMBLY: TOP COMPONENTS

32 Put glue in seat sockets, and insert spindles and arm-stumps. Orientate so best grain-figure faces forwards. Put glue into sockets in arm back-bow and bring bow down onto spindles and arm-stumps, beginning at the back. Press bow down to ensure all joints into bow go fully home. Check bow is parallel to seat surface.

PEGGING JOINTS

33 Wooden pegs may be used additionally to secure some joints, notably top and bottom of each arm-stump and the two back spindles. Drill ³⁄₁₆in (4mm) holes into joints as shown (Fig 56), and hammer in

square pegs whittled to a slightly tapered round for about two-thirds of their length. Clean off tops of pegs flush or leave a little proud.

FINISHING

34 With turned parts polished in the lathe, and seat and bow already sealed, finish chair with two or three applications of wax polish, and buff to a rich natural shine.

SMOKER'S BOW		CUTTING LIST (Add waste)			
No.	ITEM	INCHES		mm	
1	Seat	20 × 18 × 2		510 × 460 × 50	
2	(Half arms)	40 × 8 × 1½		1020 × 200 × 38	
1	(Back scroll)	17 × 5 × 5		430 × 125 × 125	
4	Legs	17½ × 2¼ × 2¼		445 × 56 × 56	
2	Stretchers	17 × 1¾ × 1¾		430 × 44 × 44	
2	Stretchers	17 × 1½ × 1½		430 × 38 × 38	
2	Arm-stumps	10½ × 1½ × 1½		265 × 38 × 38	
6	Spindles	10½ × 1⅛ × 1⅛		265 × 28 × 28	

DOUBLE BOW WINDSOR

Regarded by some as the ultimate country chair, the double bow Windsor marked a significant step forward in style and sophistication. As has been seen, the principle of the curved arm-bow or hoop was already understood and used either alone or together with the more common comb-back. Using an additional bow, or replacing the comb with a bow above the arm-bow, was a logical progression.

The first of these chairs are thought to have appeared around the mid-1770s. The 'double bow' designation tells us that it is a chair with arms, and this distinguishes it from the single bow or side chair (page 96) which, chronologically, came later. The bow-shaped stretcher which braces and strengthens the underframe is known as a 'crinoline stretcher'. This style of chair may also be seen with cabriole legs, 'Chippendale' fretted centre splats, and in mahogany; but I regard these eccentricities as totally alien to the true 'country' tradition.

Several features of this chair make it typically North of England in origin, and dating from the early nineteenth century onwards. Chairs from this area tended to be more sturdily built and perhaps a little less refined than those made further south – an example of the regional differences which exist between so many country chair styles.

All four legs of this chair are of the triple-ring and vase-foot pattern, while the bulbous arm-stumps reflect this same style of turning. The single-taper back-sticks and side-sticks, although less elegant than the double-taper sticks of other chairs, have considerable strength and add to the overall strength of the construction, as does the heavy section arm-bow.

This chair was made in ash with an elm seat, and finished in an antique dark stain before polishing. Beech could be used instead of the ash; alternatively use a fruitwood, or better still, yew, especially if polished to a natural finish.

By scaling down the given measurements, a charming child's chair may be made, as shown in the photograph opposite. Quite often in the past, chairs of this size and smaller were made as apprentice pieces, and some were used as salesmen's samples. Information about how to make this smaller version is also included here.

A nineteenth-century cottage interior with Windsor chair

Late nineteenth-century double bow Windsor

136

RECIPE

BENT COMPONENTS

1 Select and prepare material for bending the arm-bow, back-bow and crinoline stretcher.

2 Make and use the formers described in Fig 58, and refer to page 36 for steam-bending instructions.

3 Bend all components, then leave to dry and set.

SEAT: CUT OUT; MARK AND DRILL UNDERSIDE

4 Cut seat to pattern shown, using a hand-saw or bandsaw.

5 Mark out position of leg sockets on underside of seat, and draw in the alignment or sight lines. See Fig 58.

6 Drill the four leg sockets, 1in (25mm) in diameter, 1⅛in (28mm) deep to angles given in diagram; back legs 25°, front legs 10°. See page 38, or use any other method. Take care not to drill too deep, especially at front of seat because of seat hollowing which follows.

SEAT: HOLLOWING AND SHAPING

7 Mark out area of seat to be hollowed, and rough out to the drawn lines. (Refer to diagram for guide to seat profile.) Use any suitable, safe method; see page 34. Leave final finish until later.

8 Clean up edge of seat, chamfer top and bottom edges.

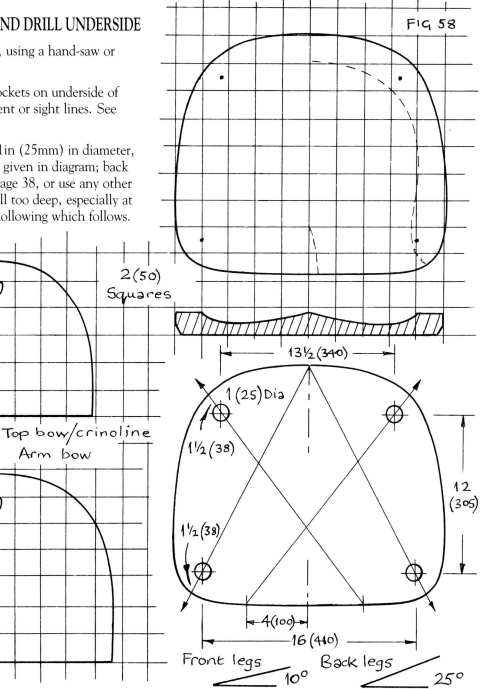

FIG 58

2(50) Squares

Formers

Top bow/crinoline
Arm bow

13½ (340)

1 (25) Dia

1½ (38)

1½ (38)

12 (305)

4 (100)

16 (410)

Front legs 10°

Back legs 25°

TURNED COMPONENTS

9 Lathe-turn the four legs, two stub-stretchers and two arm-stumps as in Fig 59. Ensure arm-stumps have sufficient 1in (25mm) parallel to pass through thickness of seat.

10 Turn, or otherwise produce the six long back-sticks and the six shorter side-sticks. Back-sticks are overlength and will require adjustment later.

CENTRE SPLAT: MARKING OUT AND CUTTING

11 Mark out centre splat to pattern shown. Make in two parts as in diagram. Length measurements are generous and will require adjustment later.

12 Cut out external and internal shapes, then clean up.

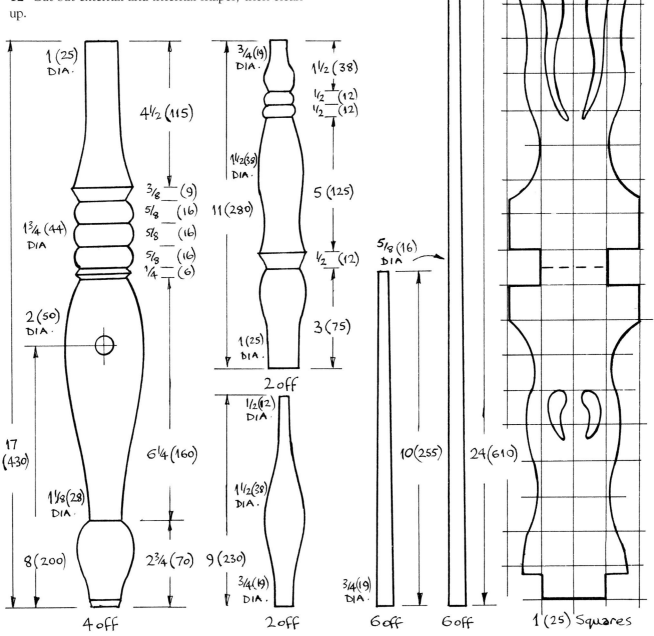

139

FITTING LEGS AND DRILLING STRETCHER SOCKETS

13 With seat upside-down on bench, fit legs into drilled sockets. Make sure they fit well and go to full depth.

14 Orientate legs so that best grain-figure faces forward.

15 Mark position of stretcher sockets on 'inside' surface of each leg (see Fig 59).

16 Mark legs and appropriate sockets for identification at reassembly; remove legs from sockets.

17 Drill stretcher sockets, all at ¾in (19mm) diameter, ¾in (19mm) deep, back legs at 18°, front legs at 6°. Refit legs into correct sockets.

22 Replace crinoline and add stub-stretchers. See Final Assembly, stage 53, and note below. Check on level surface for wobble, and adjust if necessary. When satisfied, disassemble for next stage.

NOTE: It may be necessary to adjust lengths of stretchers during trial assembly, but remember, stretchers should stretch and must be fitted under slight tension. Drilling into back curve of crinoline stretcher is best done by hand with component held in a bench vice. Take care in sighting angle of 'lie-line' when drilling.

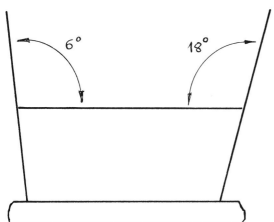

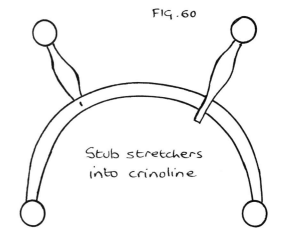

CRINOLINE STRETCHER

18 Check length of crinoline stretcher (Fig 60). Reduce both ends to ¾in (19mm) diameter. Round over inside (concave) surface of stretcher, leave outside (convex) surface square (to take stub-stretcher sockets).

19 Trial-fit stretcher into sockets in front legs; it should spring into place under slight tension and be parallel to seat.

STUB-STRETCHERS AND TRIAL ASSEMBLY

20 Whilst crinoline stretcher remains in place, insert stub-stretchers into back leg sockets and allow them to lie on crinoline (Fig 60). Mark their socket positions and 'lie-lines' as an aid to drilling at correct angle.

21 Remove crinoline and drill sockets, ½in (12mm) in diameter, ¾in (19mm) deep. Adjust length of stub-stretchers if necessary.

Assembling the underframe; fitting the crinoline stretcher

MARKING OUT AND DRILLING TOP OF SEAT (I)

23 With seat uppermost on bench, mark out position of all sockets for back-sticks, side-sticks and arm-stumps. Draw in alignment lines. Mark out position of slot mortice for centre splat. See Fig 61.

24 Drill the six back-stick sockets *only*, ¾in (19mm) in diameter, 1in (25mm) deep, at angle of 8°. (Drilling only the back-sticks at this stage is a precautionary measure in case allowances have to be made for variations in the setting of steam-bent arm-bow.)

25 Cut slot mortice for centre splat at this time also, ¼in (6mm) wide, ½in (12mm) deep, at angle of 8°.

ARM-BOW: DRILLING AND FITTING BACK-STICKS

26 Check that arm-bow has set to correct shape. It should have an internal measurement across its open ends of about 19in (480mm).

27 Mark out the six back-stick sockets on *top* surface of arm-bow. Drill these from the top, ⅝in (16mm) in diameter and right through. The drilling angle is still 8° (Fig 61).

28 Place the six back-sticks into their respective sockets in seat, and trial-fit the arm-bow down onto them.

NOTE: Some adjustment to the back-stick tapers may be required to give the bow a neat fit at 10in (250mm) above the seat surface. Alternatively, holes through arm-bow may be reamed out from below. No glue is used in this area at final assembly, and sticks should be an easy push-fit into arm-bow, without gaps at top surface of bow.

ARM-BOW: DRILLING AND FITTING SIDE-STICKS

29 With arm-bow in correct position, check relationship of arm-bow to marked positions of side-stick and arm-stump sockets on surface of seat (stage 23). Angle for drilling can be verified using a sliding (carpenter's or adjustable) bevel tool or any other means. The angle should be around 8°; use correct or corrected angle in next two stages. Disassemble sticks and bow.

30 Drill remaining sockets in seat, ¾in (19mm) in diameter, 1in (25mm) deep for side-sticks; 1in (25mm) in diameter and right through seat for arm-stumps at 8° (or other angle).

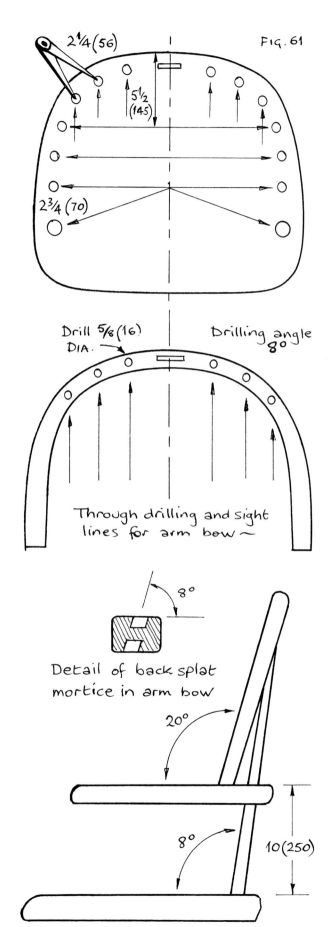

FIG. 61

2¼ (56)

5½ (145)

2¾ (70)

Drill ⅝ (16) DIA.

Drilling angle 8°

Through drilling and sight lines for arm bow ~

8°

Detail of back splat mortice in arm bow

20°

8°

10 (250)

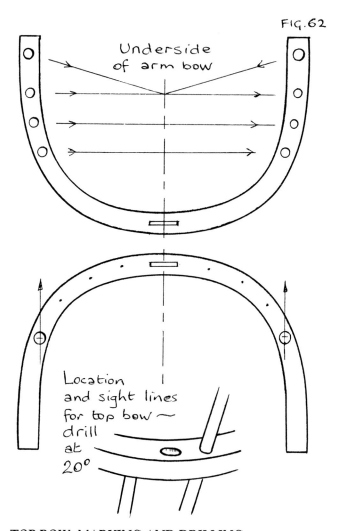

FIG. 62

Underside of arm bow

Location and sight lines for top bow — drill at 20°

31 Mark out *underside* of arm-bow for side-stick and arm-stump sockets (Fig 62). Socket spacing as in Fig 61.

32 Arm-bow is drilled from underside, which means drilling alignment is now reverse of previous drilling to give correct orientation.

33 Drill side-stick sockets ⅝in (16mm) in diameter, ¾in (19mm) deep; and arm-stump sockets ¾in (19mm) in diameter, ⅞in (22mm) deep, at angle of 8° (or other angle). Note these do not go through arm-bow.

34 Mark out and cut slot mortices for back-splat in top and underside of arm-bow. They should be at the 8° angle (refer back to Fig 61).

NOTE: These do not go through arm-bow either.

ARM-BOW: FINAL TRIAL-FIT

35 Try side-sticks, arm-stumps and lower part of back-splat for individual fit. Check that arm-stumps protrude through seat. Leave all in position.

36 Refit back-sticks, and lower arm-bow down into position, manipulating side-sticks, etc into sockets in underside of arm-bow. Check height of arm-bow at 10in (250mm) parallel above seat.

FITTING TOP BOW IN ARM-BOW

37 With arm-bow, etc remaining in place, mark position of sockets for top bow in arm-bow, and check angle and alignment carefully. (See note below.)

38 Remove arm-bow and drill these two sockets, ¾in (19mm) in diameter, ¾in (19mm) deep, at angle of 20°. Refit arm-bow (Fig 62).

39 Reduce ends of top bow to ¾in (19mm) in diameter and fit fully into sockets in arm-bow. Top bow should be sprung in under tension.

40 Allow back-sticks, which are overlength at this stage, to lie temporarily to front or back of top bow.

NOTE: Check angle and alignment for top-bow socket drilling very carefully, and allow for some tension in bow when assembling. It is important that these sockets do not come too close to back- or side-stick sockets, as arm-bow will be severely weakened if they do. Ideally they should be midway between last back-stick and first side-stick (Fig 62).

TOP BOW: MARKING AND DRILLING

41 With everything still in place, locate top centre of top bow and mark position of slot mortice for central splat on it.

42 Back-sticks are arranged equally spaced to each side of this at approximately 2⅜in (59mm) centres, as in Fig 63. Mark their positions on inside (concave) surface of bow. Mark 'lie' of each back-stick on front surface of bow.

43 Ascertain required length for each individual back-stick. Identify components. Disassemble bows and back-sticks.

44 Cut back-sticks to length, and check joint areas for size.

45 Drill sockets for back-sticks in underside (concave) surface of top bow, ½in (12mm) in diameter, ½in (12mm) deep. Drilling angle may vary, but should be around 12°. (This stage relies much on eye judgement, but see page 39 and Fig 34 on page 101 for help with drilling back-stick sockets in top bows.)

46 Cut centre-splat mortice slot at same angle.

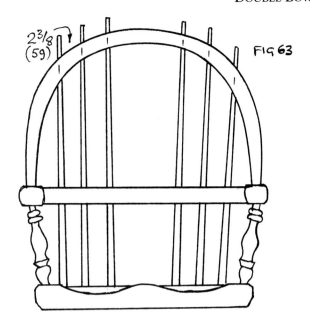

Fitting the back-splat into the top bow

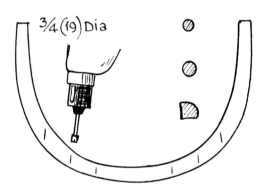

TOP COMPONENTS: FINAL TRIAL ASSEMBLY

47 Refit back-sticks, etc, and add arm-bow to correct height above seat.

48 Put top part of centre splat in position; adjust length if necessary.

49 Enter top bow into arm-bow sockets, and manipulate back-sticks and centre splat into top-bow sockets, bringing everything down to a good fit. Be especially sure that top-bow tenons go to full depth in arm-bow sockets. Make any necessary adjustments, and when satisfied, check that components are orientated for best grain-figure and marked for identification. Then disassemble.

FINAL SHAPING AND CLEANING UP

50 Complete work on seat hollowing, then remove all tool marks and bring to a smooth finish.

51 Shape and clean up arm-bow and top bow to profiles shown in Fig 63.

52 Clean up and smooth all other components; do not touch well-fitting joints.

NOTE: If the chair is to be stained (as this one was), all finishing should be left until after assembly. If it is to be left a natural colour, components can be sealed and sanded before assembly (see page 41). Remember to keep sealer off joint areas.

FINAL ASSEMBLY: UNDERFRAME

53 With seat upside-down on protected bench, put glue into leg sockets in seat, and into stretcher sockets in legs and crinoline stretcher. Insert legs part-way into appropriate seat sockets, put crinoline stretcher in place, add stub-stretchers, and push or tap everything into place and to full depth. Stand on level surface and check stability.

FINAL ASSEMBLY: TOP COMPONENTS

54 Make saw-cuts into bottom of arm-stumps for wedging; see page 47. Make wedges.

55 Put glue into back-splat mortice, also back-stick, side-stick and arm-stump sockets in seat surface. Insert all these components, orientating back- and side-sticks for best grain-figure. Check that arm-stump wedge saw-cuts lie *across* grain of seat.

56 Put glue in arm-stump and side-stick sockets, and in back-splat mortice in underside of arm-bow. No glue in back-stick sockets. Slide arm-bow down over back-sticks and onto components arising from seat. Tap down to full depth, and 10in (250mm) parallel above seat.

57 Invert onto protected bench, and tap wedges into arm-stumps. Wipe off surplus glue.

58 Stand chair on legs again, and put glue into back-

143

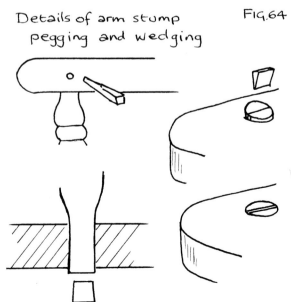

The final assembly of the chair

59 Cut arm-stump and wedge protrusions flush with underside of seat. Additionally, secure top joint of arm-stumps and centre back-splat by pegging. See Fig 64.

FINISHING

60 For a natural finish, if previously sealed and sanded, clean off any marks and apply a good quality wax polish. For a dark stained and polished finish, refer to page 42.

CHILD'S CHAIR

61 To make this version of the chair, I worked to a basic two-thirds scale, or 66.6 per cent of the original dimensions. Odd decimal fractions are rounded up to a convenient working measurement.

62 This gives a seat size, for example, of 13½in (340mm) by 11½in (290mm), and leg lengths of 11½in (290mm). Leg diameters become 1⅜in (35mm) with ⅞in (22mm) joints into seat; back-stick diameters ½in (12mm) at bottom, ⁷⁄₁₆in (10.5mm) at arm-bow, ⅜in (9mm) at top.

63 Drilling angles do not change, but remain as in the full-size version.

splat mortice and top-bow sockets in top of arm-bow. Put glue into back-stick sockets and splat mortice in top bow. Add top part of back-splat to arm-bow, place top bow into position, and manipulate back-sticks and splat up into it whilst bringing top bow down to full depth in arm-bow sockets. Tap everything into place and check all is correctly assembled. Wipe off surplus glue and allow to set.

Details of arm stump pegging and wedging   FIG.64

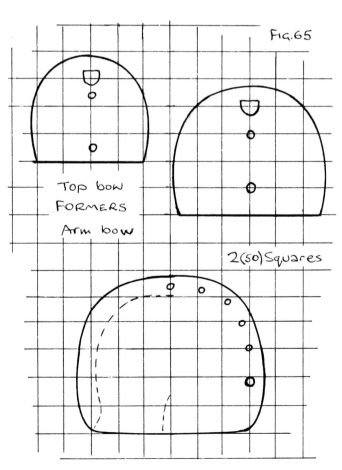

FIG.65

Top bow FORMERS

Arm bow

2(50) Squares

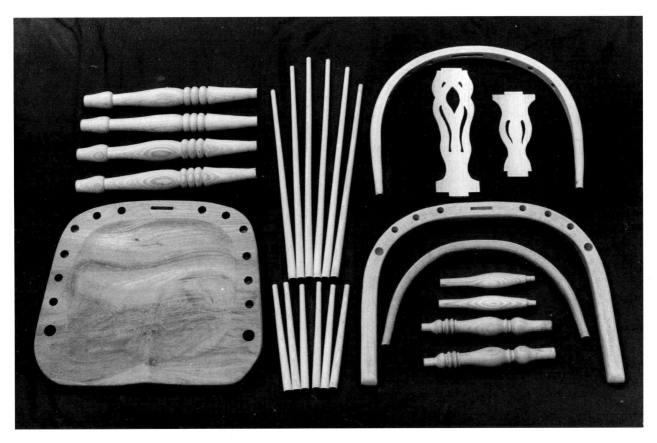

Double bow Windsor chair parts

64 Different formers will have to be made for the bent components. See Fig 65.

65 The small chair shown differs from the original in two ways: it has no back-slat, and does not have a

crinoline stretcher. These are a matter of personal choice.

66 Fig 65 will be found helpful in making the new formers, drawing the seat shape, and in marking out for back-sticks only. Similar stick spacings will repeat on the arm-bow and underside of top bow.

DOUBLE BOW		CUTTING LIST (Add waste)	
No.	ITEM	INCHES	mm
1	Seat	20 × 18 × 1¾	510 × 460 × 44
4	Legs	17 × 2 × 2	430 × 50 × 50
1	(for arm-bow)	48 × 1½ × 1½	1220 × 38 × 38
1	(for top-bow)	43 × 1⅛ × 1⅛	1090 × 28 × 28
1	(for crinoline)	30 × 1⅛ × 1⅛	760 × 28 × 28
2	Arm stumps	11 × 1½ × 1½	280 × 38 × 38
2	Stub-stretchers	9 × 1½ × 1½	230 × 38 × 38
6	Back-sticks	24 × ¾ × ¾	610 × 19 × 19
6	Side-sticks	10 × ¾ × ¾	255 × 19 × 19
1	Back-splat	24 × 4 × ⅜	610 × 100 × 9

Glossary

Adze	Cutting tool with a curved, dished blade at right angles to its long curved handle. Used to hollow chair seats, etc.
Annual Rings	(See Growth Rings)
Beetle	Short-handled heavy mallet used to strike an axe or wedge when cleaving.
Bending Strap	Metal strap with end stops used to restrain the fibres of wood during steam bending.
Bevel	(See Chamfer, Sliding Bevel)
Billet	Short sawn section of tree trunk or the roughly shaped piece split from it and made ready for the lathe (depending on the region).
Bodger	Late-nineteenth-century term for woodland chair-leg turners.
Bookmatching	Matching-up wood grain by cutting and exposing adjacent surfaces as in opening the pages of a book.
Bow	Curved, usually steam bent, component of a chair; either arm bow or back bow.
Brake	Several kinds of home-made vice or holding devices are known as brakes.
Chamfer	Narrow angled surface along an edge or corner. Also bevel.
Cleave	To split wood along the grain.
Comb	Top rail of chair, into which back sticks are socketed. Also cresting rail.
Cramp (clamp)	Device for holding or applying pressure to wood. Various types including 'G' cramp (US 'C' clamp), sash cramp, etc.
Donkey	Alternative name for shaving horse.
Drawknife	Two-handled knife-like tool, drawn towards the user. Used to trim excess wood quickly.
Dry run	Initial assembly of components without glue.
Fan Back	Type of chair in which the comb is wider than the seat, causing the back sticks to fan outwards.
Former (form)	Mould upon which wood is held to bend it to shape.
Froe	Cleaving tool with blade at right angles to handle. Used in the controlled splitting of coppice material.
Glue-up	Gluing and assembly stage.
Grain	The direction and arrangement of the fibrous tissues in wood; the surface pattern or texture resulting from this.
Growth Rings	Concentric layers of wood tissue increasing the girth of growing trees.
Inshave	Two-handed tool resembling a deeply curved drawknife used for chair seat hollowing.
In Wind	Refers to wood or assembled components which are twisted or out of shape (pronounced as in kind).

Jig	Any device used to hold or locate components or tools for processing or to aid repetitive work.
Legging-up	The process of fitting chair legs and stretchers.
Moisture Content	The proportion of moisture in wood expressed as a percentage.
Mortice	A recess, usually rectangular, cut into wood to receive a matching tenon. Here, round 'mortice and tenons' are used. (See Tenon)
Poppets	The two short uprights on a pole lathe between which the workpiece is rotated.
Rail	Horizontal chair component, eg, seat rail, back rail.
Rake	To incline or be inclined from the vertical.
Rising Grain	The way in which the grain (figure) of turned components rises upwards in a series of arches.
Rotary Plane	(See Rounder)
Rounder	More commonly used name for rotary plane – a tool used to 'turn' wood by hand or machine.
Saddle	Descriptive term used to describe chair seat hollowing.
Shaving Horse	A holding device.
Side Axe	Flat-sided axe sharpened on opposite side only and used for the close trimming of green wood.
Side Chair	Chair without arms, also called a single chair.
Slat Back	American name for a ladderback chair.
Sliding Bevel	Adjustable carpenters' 'square' used to mark-out or check angles.
Splat	Decorated, pierced upright in centre of English Windsor chairs. Also called baluster.
Stail Engine	Stail; old name for any long, straight, round handle: engine; from the Latin, meaning ingenious device: hence, a tool for making long, turned, round handles.
Sticks	The vertical, round-tapered components in Windsor chair backs.
Stretchers	The horizontal components which connect and strengthen chair legs.
Tenon	The 'male' part of a mortice and tenon joint. (See Mortice)
Torque	A force which causes or tends to cause rotation.
Travisher	Traditional tool used after the adze in chair seat hollowing.
Uprights	Main vertical components on open frame chairs.
'V' cradle	Device for holding round components.
Waney Edge	The natural (bark) edge of a sawn board.
Wind	(See In Wind)

SUPPLIERS AND OTHER INFORMATION

TIMBER

The addresses given are of sawmills and merchants with whom I deal personally; they have good quality material and will supply small as well as large quantities. There are other sawmills and other merchants – check your local area. Also, seek out local sources of coppice and round log material from Forestry Commission, National Trust and private estate woodlands, fencing and firewood dealers, and farmers.

John Boddy Timber   Riverside Sawmills, Boroughbridge, North Yorkshire YO5 9LJ. Tel: 0423 322370
Home-grown and imported timber. Mainly kiln-dried, sawn boards but air-dried English ash available
Craft Supplies Ltd   The Mill, Miller's Dale, Derbyshire SK17 8SN. Tel: 0298 871636
Home-grown and imported timber – air- and kiln-dried. Machining service.
Paul Martin   Stocklands Farm, Staplecross, East Sussex TN32 5RT. Tel: 058 083 0267
Locally grown hardwoods, air- and kiln-dried. Machining service
Milland Fine Timber Ltd   Rakers Yard, Milland, Liphook, Hampshire GU30 7JS. Tel: 0428 76505
Home-grown hardwoods; kiln-dried and air-dried sawn timber. Machining service
W.L. West & Sons Ltd   Selham, Petworth, West Sussex GU28 0PJ. Tel: 079 85611
Home-grown and European timber. Air-dried and kiln-dried timber stocks
Henry Venables   Doxey Road, Stafford, Staffordshire SD16 2EN. Tel: 0785 55115
Kiln-dried home-grown and European timber stocks
Bill Wilder   Church Farm, Easton Grey, Malmesbury, Wiltshire SN16 0PF. Tel: 0666 840254
Locally grown hardwoods, air- and kiln-dried. Machining service

SEATING MATERIALS

John Excell   The Cane Workshop, Gospel Hall, Westport, Langport, Somerset TA10 0BH. Tel: 0460 281636
Jacobs, Young & Westbury Ltd   Bridge Road, Haywards Heath, West Sussex RH16 1UA. Tel: 0444 412411

FINISHING MATERIALS

John Myland Ltd   80 Norwood High Street, London SE27 9NW. Tel: 071 670 9161
Pine Brush Products   Stockingate, Coton Clanford, Stafford ST18 9PB. Tel: 0785 282799
Rustins Ltd   Waterloo Road, Cricklewood, London NW2 7TX. Tel: 081 450 4666.

TOOLS

Ashem Crafts, 2 Oakleigh Avenue, Hallow, Worcester, Worcestershire WR2 6NG. Tel: 0905 640070
Sole manufacturer and supplier of the Fred Lambert rotary planes or rounders and trapping plane, as described and used in this book. Made in a range of sizes both English imperial and metric. Also available, the gearbox rounding machine, complete and with accessories, or the separate components to make your own machine. All tools are available singly, but the following basic 'set' is recommended for chairmaking:
1¼in rounder
1⅜in rounder
1in rounder
¾in rounder   ⎫ Required for Windsor
½in rounder   ⎬ back spindles only
Standard trapping plane   ⎭
Ashley Iles (Edge Tools) Ltd   East Kirby, Spilsby, Lincolnshire PE23 4DD. Tel: 0790 3372
Gouges and chisels for wood-turning and carving
Boddy's Fine Wood and Tool Store   Boroughbridge, North Yorkshire YO5 9LJ. Tel: 0423 322370
General tools, including hand adze and inshave. Finishing materials
Bristol Design (Tools) Ltd   14, Perry Road, Bristol BS1 5BG. Tel: 0272 291740
Quality used tools and new specialist tools including adze, side axe, froe and travisher blades
Clico (Sheffield) Tooling Ltd   Fell Road Industrial Estate, Sheffield, Yorkshire S9 2AL. Tel: 0742 433007
Quality specialist tools including Forstner bits, spoon bits, curved sole spokeshaves, chairmaker's slot mortice bits
Craft Supplies Ltd   The Mill, Miller's Dale, Derbyshire SK17 8SN. Tel: 0298 871636
Wood-turning tools and accessories. Finishing materials

CHAIRMAKING COURSES

Jack Hill Workshops   PO Box 20, Midhurst, West Sussex GU29 0JD. Tel: 0730 813368
Traditional chairmaking and C & G furniture courses and demonstrations held at own workshop and at other venues. Chair plans and other publications from Craftwork Publications at same address
Living Wood Training, Mike Abbot   159 Cotswold Road, Windmill Hill, Bristol BS3 4PH. Tel: 0272 636244
Green wood and chairmaking courses and demonstrations
West Dean College   West Dean, Chichester, West Sussex PO18 0QZ. Tel: 0243 63301
Short crafts courses including chairmaking and seat weaving
Buckinghamshire College of Higher Education   High Wycombe, Bucks HP11 2JZ. Tel: 0494 522141
Traditional chairmaking included in full-time furniture courses

ORGANISATIONS

Tools and Trades History Society   Secretary, 60 Swanley Lane, Swanley, Kent
Regional Furniture Society   Secretary, Townley Hall, Burnley, Lancashire
Green Wood Trust   Rose Cottage, Dale Road, Coalbrookdale, Telford, Shropshire
Association of Woodturners of Great Britain   Secretary, 5 Kent Gardens, Eastcoate, Ruislip, Middlesex
Irish Woodturners Guild   Secretary, Spiddal Craft Centre, Spiddal, Co Galway, Ireland
Association of Pole Lathe Turners   Secretary, Carreg Rhys, Paradwys, Bodorgan, Ynys Mon, Gwynedd
British Trust for Conservation Volunteers   Balby Road, Doncaster, Yorks

PLACES TO VISIT

Local History and Chair Museum   Castle Hill House, Priory Avenue, High Wycombe, Bucks
Chairs, local history, chairmakers' tools and workshop
Amgueddfa Werin Cymru, Welsh Folk Museum   St Fagans, Cardiff, Wales
Furniture and chairs, cottage interiors
Ulster Folk Museum   Cultra, Holywood, Belfast, Northern Ireland
Furniture and chairs, artefacts, cottage interiors, demonstrations
Highland Folk Museum   Kingussie, Inverness, Scotland
Furniture, chairs, local history
American Museum in Britain   Claverton Manor, Bath, Somerset
Colonial and Shaker furniture and chairs in room settings
Cotswold Country Museum   Arlington Mill, Bibury, Gloucestershire
Arts and Crafts Furniture, including work by Gimson
West Yorkshire Folk Museum   Shibden Hall, Halifax, Yorkshire
Tools and artefacts, chairs, craft workshops
Leicester City Museum   Leicester, Leicestershire
Gimson- and Clissett-style chairs
City Museum   St Albans, Hertfordshire
Collection of tools, including chairmakers' tools
Museum of English Rural Life   Whiteknights Park, Reading, Berkshire
Tools, artefacts, woodland and coppice crafts displays
Weald and Downland Museum   Singleton, Chichester, W. Sussex
Woodland and coppice crafts displays and demonstrations
Practical Woodworking Exhibition   Wembley, London
Annually, February/March. Tool and timber suppliers, demonstrations
Woodworker Exhibition   Sandown Park, Surrey
Annually, September/October. Tool and timber suppliers, demonstrations

PHOTOGRAPH CREDITS

Acknowledgement is gratefully given to the following for assistance in obtaining and permission to reproduce illustrations. Every attempt has been made to credit copyright holders, but the author offers apologies in advance for any errors or omissions.

P8, p9, p66 Victoria and Albert Museum; p10 American Museum in Britain; p12, p104, p136 Dr Bernard Cotton; p13, p14 (top), p72, p128 High Wycombe Chair Museum; p14 (bottom), p15, p16, p17, p34 (bottom) Museum of English Rural Life; p21 Forestry Commission; p56, p80 (left) Welsh Folk Museum; p80 (right) Worksop Library; p88 Cheltenham Museum; p114 Rosemary Stuart-Jones.

The remaining black and white photographs are by the author; processed by Michael Chevis.

The pole lathe and outdoor workshop

ACKNOWLEDGEMENTS

To the generations of largely unknown and unpretentious craftsmen who developed the chairs which I now make, and who established the standard of honest workmanship to which I aspire, I owe a debt of gratitude. Likewise to those who influenced me 'as a lad' when I was but a raw apprentice, I say 'thank you'.

In later life, after I had done other things in other places, Fred Lambert inspired my interest in woodland crafts in general and in traditional chairmaking in particular, and it was he who encouraged me to learn and practise the skills of the rural craftsmen and to teach others how to do so. With Fred, who sadly died in 1989, I served my second apprenticeship, and for that I shall always be grateful.

Thanks must also go to my many friends, fellow craftsmen and associates both in and out of 'the trade', and to the students of all ages and both sexes who, in colleges and on courses, keep me actively (and gainfully) employed from time to time, benefiting, I hope, from the mutual experience of knowledge shared and the guided practice of skills.

I acknowledge, too, both early and more recent writers whose work concerning the history and development of chairs and chairmaking, and the tools and working methods of the craftsmen involved, has certainly helped me. For the benefit of others, these sources are listed in the bibliography.

Many of the illustrations of an historical nature came from the archives of various institutions and individuals, and relevant credits are given elsewhere. I greatly appreciate the help given. And in the making of the book I should like to thank the publishers for their patience. And mine.

Individually I would like to thank John Plimmer for his inspired colour photography of the chairs which I have made and for the jacket illustration; West Dean College; Jenny and Jim Collier and Rosemary Stuart-Jones who kindly provided the locations for the photography; Wendy Manser for rushing my chair seats so well; Linda for word processing all my hand-written pages; and lastly a special thank-you to Fran, without whose help the book would probably never have been written.

I can make a chair from a tree But only God can make a tree

150

SELECTED BIBLIOGRAPHY

Abbott, Mike *Green Woodwork* (GMC Publications, 1989)

Alexander, J.D. *Make a Chair from a Tree* (Taunton Press, 1978)

Arnold, J. *The Countryman's Workshop* (Phoenix House, 1953; EP Publications, 1977*)

Arnold, J. *Shell Book of Country Crafts* (John Baker 1968, 1970, 1974, 1977*)

Bishop, Robert *The American Chair* (Bonanza Books, 1972, 1983*)

Brown, John *Welsh Stick Chairs* (Abercastle Publications, 1990)

Brown, Margery *Cane and Rush Seating* (Batsford, 1976, 1977)

Carruthers, A. (Ed) *Ernest Gimson and the Cotswold Group* (Leicestershire Museums Publication, No 14, 1978)

Cotton, Dr Bernard 'Country Chairs and their Makers' *Collectors' Guide, 1983*

Cotton, Dr Bernard *The English Regional Chair* (Antique Collectors Club, 1990)

Desch, H.E. *Timber: Its Structure and Properties* (Macmillan, 1938, 4th edition 1968*)

Dunbar, Michael *Make a Windsor Chair* (Taunton Press, 1984)

Edlin, Herbert *Woodland Crafts in Britain* (Batsford, 1949; David & Charles 1974*)

Edlin, Herbert *Trees, Woods and Man* (Collins, 1956, 1966, 1970*)

Fitzrandolph, H.E. and Hay, M.D. *The Rural Industries of England and Wales, Vol 1* (Oxford University Press, 1926; E.P. Publications, 1977*)

Gloag, John *The Englishman's Chair* (Allen & Unwin, 1964*)

Hill, Jack *Complete Practical Book of Country Crafts* (David & Charles, 1979, 1980, 1981, 1983*)

— — 'Country Chairs and Chairmaking' *Woodworker* March, April, May, July, September 1980

— — 'In The Coppice' *Woodworker* July 1981

— — 'Making a Shaving Horse' *Working Wood* Vol 3, No 4, 1982

— — *Making Family Heirlooms* (David & Charles, 1985, 1988, 1992)

— — 'Steam Bending' *Practical Woodworking* June 1986

— — 'The Chairmaker's' *Woodworking International* April 1987

— — 'Green Stool Project' *Practical Woodworking* March 1988

Holdstock, R. *Seat Weaving in Rush, Cane and Cord* (GMC Publications, 1989)

Jenkins, J.G. *Traditional Country Craftsmen* (RKP, 1965, 1978*)

Lambert, Fred *Tools and Devices for Coppice Crafts* (Evens Bros/Young Farmers Club booklet, 1957*. Photocopy edition available from Craftwork Publications, PO Box 20, Midhurst, W Sussex)

Loudon, J.C. *Furniture Designs from the Encyclopedia of Cottage, Farm and Villa Architecture, 1839* (Reprint SR Publishers Ltd, 1970*)

Mayes, L.J. *The History of Chairmaking in High Wycombe* (RKP, 1960*)

Moser, Thomas *Windsor Chairmaking* (Stirling, 1982)

Muller, C.R. and Rieman, T.D. *The Shaker Chair* (Canal Press, 1984)

Sparkes, Ivan *The English Country Chair* (Spurbooks, 1973*)

— — *The Windsor Chair* (Spurbooks, 1975*)

— — *English Domestic Furniture, 1100–1837* (Spurbooks, 1980*)

— — *Woodland Craftsmen* (Shire Album No 25, 1977, 1991)

— — *English Windsor Chairs* (Shire Album No 70, 1981, 1985)

Stevens, W.C. and Turner, N. *Solid and Laminated Wood Bending* (HMSO 1948. Revised 1970*, reprinted as *Wood Bending Handbook* [Woodcraft Supply Corp, 1989])

Several of these titles are now out of print (*). Most of the others are available from Stobart Davies, Priory House, Priory Street, Hartford, SG14 1RN.

INDEX